T0077935

REBEL WITHOUT APPLAUSE

DONALD STEELE PH.D.

authorHOUSE®

AuthorHouse™
1663 Liberty Drive
Bloomington, IN 47403
www.authorhouse.com
Phone: 1 (800) 839-8640

Published by AuthorHouse 11/06/2020

ISBN: 978-1-7283-4859-9 (sc)
ISBN: 978-1-7283-4861-2 (hc)

Cover Art: Forrest Miller
www.facebook.com/ForrestMillerArt

Print information available on the last page.

PREFACE

This is a family business legacy story. While this book features the life and times of Jon Hall, founder and CEO of Glastender, Inc., an industry-leading food equipment manufacturing firm, there is a clear underlying message: A multi-generational family business legacy is bigger than one individual.

Jon's life is atypical in ways that will inspire those who think you need a Harvard University degree to create a successful business that can survive and thrive across multiple generations, overcoming numerous challenges along the way.

Jon Hall has followed the personal path to happiness that reminds me of an ideology written by the author of 25 highly acclaimed business books, David Cottrell:

> *Happiness comes from following your passion. Excellence comes from work you are passionate about.*
> *Knowing what to do is certainly important but knowing why you do it fuels your motivation ... your passion.*
> *A strong passion enables you to find a way to achieve your goals ... any goal.*

Passion turns your stumbling blocks into stepping stones. Not only does passion ignite your pursuit of excellence, passion also makes the journey more fun!

Today at Glastender, over 215 employees keep the place humming. In addition to adding square feet to the factory, many other changes have been implemented:

- Continued investments in state-of-the art equipment. A key element in the quality of Glastender's products and in its efficiency in manufacturing is the use of leading-edge automated sheet metal processing equipment.
- Many improvements with respect to the human side of the business. Initiatives have been launched that contribute to a shared sense of duty, unity, and of common interests and responsibilities. Employees are truly engaged.

"Doing it first or doing it better" is the mantra that drives the Glastender business engine. Jon pioneered a sense of creativity, flexibility, and feature focus. When Jay Kegerreis came on as a minority business partner, he brought with him a Wake Forest University economics degree, which added a business acumen that was missing. The second generation of Glastender leadership has taken the business to a whole new professional level that maintains a focus on best practices.

Jon offers a warning to all who aspire to be entrepreneurs: it is not for the lazy or the meek. "All my life, I have only worked half-days — 12 hours a day. And while the third beatitude from Jesus's Sermon on the Mount says, "The meek shall inherit the earth,' that's probably the only way they'll get it!"

ACKNOWLEDGMENTS

Glastender Inc., founded in 1969 by Jon Hall, is celebrating its 50th anniversary. This second-generation food equipment manufacturing business has grown into a world-class business that enjoys a truly engaged workforce led by an experienced and highly effective leadership team. Capturing the legacy of Jon Hall and the business he founded has proven to be an enlightening historical discourse that discloses the unique path that Jon Hall and his family took as it molded and shaped the successful family-owned and -operated business venture Glastender, Inc. is today.

I have so many people to thank for their willingness to contribute to my authorship of this book. Clearly, the Hall family has given freely of its time and talents to make sure that I got what I needed and when I needed it. Having known Jon for over 70 years, I have come to realize that I didn't really know him nearly as well as I thought I did. Hardly anybody does.

Kim Hall Norris has been especially helpful in several ways: interviewing her dad, suggesting others for me to interview, and providing editorial help for which I am truly grateful. Todd Hall provided the initial video presentation during which he interviewed his father. This gave me an initial set of understandings that got me started off on the right foot. He also contributed a chapter that required a depth of understanding of the Glastender operations that I lacked.

Rejeana Heinrich, associate director of the Stevens Center for Family Business, contributed an in-depth chapter on family business and was always ready to provide insights, editing, and motivational encouragement.

Dr. Don Bachand, president of Saginaw Valley State University, afforded me the opportunity to work as his special assistant for professional development and the opportunity to teach Business and Management classes to graduating seniors at SVSU. The access I was granted enabled me to gain insights from Dr. Anthony Bowrin, dean of the College of Business and Management; Chairman Mazen Jaber; Professor Izabella Szymanska; and other faculty members. Their individual and collective insights were very helpful to me in my role as a family business legacy author.

Finally, I want to thank Jon Hall for his willingness to discuss his wins and losses along the way. His most heartfelt loss came with the premature death of his best friend and business partner, Jay Kegerreis. Jon is reluctant to talk too deeply about his past successes as he is always looking forward. This makes sense when one considers the following quote from Henry David Thoreau that says, "Success usually comes to those who are too busy to be looking for it."

INTRODUCTION

Shortly after the book *Undefeated* that I had co-written with Jean Beach was released by Author House Publishing, I received a call from Kim Norris, the daughter of Jon Hall. Kim told me that she had enjoyed reading *Undefeated* and asked if I would be interested in writing a book about her father and his family-owned and -operated business. Kim quickly explained that her father was Jon Hall and that he was the founder and CEO of Glastender, Inc. Kim wanted the book written so that the family's future generations could know the legacy of Jon and the Glastender enterprise. I realized immediately that Jon Hall had been a friend and a schoolmate of mine.

Shortly after Kim's call, we agreed on a plan to move forward with a book that would capture the legacy of Jon Hall and the business he founded that is now a leading player in the food equipment manufacturing domain. I further suggested that the book could have meaning to a much larger audience of family business owners and entrepreneurs. Kim suggested I interview Rejeana Heinrich, director of the Stevens Center for Family Business at Saginaw Valley State University (SVSU). Rejeana asked me if I would be interested in speaking at the upcoming Stevens Center for Family Business event attended by members representing 86 Great Lakes Bay region family business enterprises.

I accepted Rejeana's invitation and asked Chris Shepler to join me in presenting how the book idea emerged out of a year-long succession planning, coaching, and consulting engagement I had completed with the Shepler family.

In gearing up to write the legacy story of Jon Hall and Glastender, Inc., the business he founded, I reflected on my past knowledge of Jon. Jon and I had attended St. Andrew High School in Saginaw, Michigan, and I remembered him as a unique and creative guy.

However, we hadn't crossed paths for many years, except for one class reunion gathering and a few other brief chance encounters at restaurants, such as Wally's Supper Club on Pierson Road near Flint or at Jake's Old City Grill on Saginaw's west side. My thoughts drifted back in time to 1955, the year Jon Hall and I entered the ninth grade at St. Andrew High School. This was a time of great social change in America. Much of this change was captured in the Warner Bros. movie, *Rebel Without a Cause*, starring James Dean, Sal Mineo, and Natalie Wood.

Rebel Without a Cause was released on October 27, 1955. Unlike earlier films that depicted teenagers as delinquents in urban slum environments, this movie offered a social commentary about emotionally-confused suburban middle-class teenagers, a critique of parenting of that era, and it explored the differences between generations.

James Dean played the lead role as James Stark in the movie. Unfortunately, he died before the movie was released when he crashed his Porsche sports car in California while driving at excessive speeds. Despite his tragic death at the age of 24, he became a cultural icon as the symbolic representation of teenage disillusionment and social estrangement.

In 1990, *Rebel Without a Cause* was added to the Library of Congress's National Film Registry. The movie was deemed "culturally, historically, and aesthetically significant."

Looking back I can see how, in many ways, Jon was the James Dean of our class. My comparison of Jon with James Dean derives from the perspective that both were outliers to their school cultures, and early adopters of the dramatically-changing social values that evolved during the fifties and early sixties.

While Jon had classic good looks, an athletic build, and a pleasant personality, he wasn't well-understood at home or at school; didn't particularly like school; had a small circle of friends; chose not to participate in athletics; sported a flat-top haircut (duck-tailed in the back); and loved to modify trains and bicycles and drive his souped-up hot rod cars. While he didn't die in a car crash like James Dean, he did lose his driver's license at the age of eighteen because of the many speeding tickets he had aggregated.

The major difference between Jon and James Dean is that while the role James Dean played brought him iconic status, the role Jon played was, and still is, very much under the radar of applause and fame. The rare exceptions to this phenomenon are found in Jon's highly-respected talents in the food manufacturing industry and in the hot rod world, both of which fuel his creative energies. In the food equipment manufacturing domain, Jon's name and his Glastender business shine as brightly as the stainless steel products Glastender manufactures. Similarly, in the hot rod domain, Jon has gained national attention in industry magazines such as *Street Rodder* and *Street Rods* for his well-crafted and attention-getting hot rods.

Outside of those two areas of Jon's life, he has worked in relative anonymity as he and his family have molded and shaped the industry-leading family-owned and -operated business. Even in his home town of Saginaw, Michigan, he and his Glastender business have remained virtually unknown to most people.

In interviews with Saginaw folks, I found both Jon and Glastender to be like valuable pearls hidden by the cover of a clam shell. Jon attributes his personality's lack of visibility and recognition to his rigorous and focused work schedule.

Jon was born in 1940, prior to the baby boom era that followed the end of World War II in 1945. While the children of the baby boomers were the center of most parents' lives, that was not the case with the pre-baby boomers. Jon's parents and school teachers paid little attention to the things he was most interested in as he engaged himself in the creative work of modifying his toys and, later, vehicles.

I am writing a story that hopefully captures the legacy of Jon Hall and the family business which he founded in 1969. It is intended to be informative, educational, and provocative, with the goal of bringing awareness to one man's quest to build a successful multi-generational, family-owned and -operated business. This unusual story is also intended to inspire and guide others who own and operate (or desire to own and operate) their own family business enterprise.

Rebel Without Applause also targets those college students who will choose to earn their living working as non-family employees in family-owned businesses. This is a high likelihood for many college graduates because family-owned and family-controlled firms account for approximately 70 to 80% of all incorporated businesses in the United States, wherein approximately 17 million family firms (including sole proprietorships) operate. Perhaps, most importantly, over 80% of the United States workforce is employed by family businesses and 80% of American millionaires own family businesses. For these reasons, it is beneficial for everyone seeking employment to know all they can about the opportunities and challenges that family-owned and -operated businesses offer. When requesting the book be written, Kim's main reason was for the Hall family's future generations to be aware of Jon's legacy.

In my teaching role in the College of Business and Management at SVSU, I emphasize these facts to encourage students to gain a deeper understanding of the challenges and opportunities associated with owning and/or working in a family-owned business. I sincerely believe Jon Hall's story is particularly relevant today in a world where far too little attention is given to the unique challenges faced by family businesses and to the great possibilities for success that family-owned and -operated businesses can bring.

Those who have embarked on the entrepreneurial family business journey successfully have a legacy story worth telling. If these legacies are not shared, valuable histories will be lost to future generations of family, employees, and customers. The dearth of such legacy stories is surprising because family-owned and -operated businesses are clearly the backbone of the American free enterprise system.

Chapter One

THE REBEL'S STORY

G lastender, Inc. evolved from Equipment Distributing Company (EDC), a business Jon's father founded in 1954 and eventually included sons Bill and Jon as partners.

Glastender traces its origin to 1969 when Jon invented the world's first automatic rotary glass washer, which he called a "glastender" (a play on the word bartender*)*. This invention saved space and eliminated wasted steps for bartenders. It was 1973 when Jon created Glastender as an independent entity. It was 1974 when Jon registered his company name as Glastender, Inc.

While Glastender could be viewed as the second evolution of the EDC family business enterprise, Jon considered Glastender to be a start-up, the difference being the shift from a company distributing products manufactured by others to a manufacturing business that distributes its own products. Out of respect for his father and their existing partnership in EDC, Jon made his father an equal partner in Glastender.

It was 1982 when Jon commenced a five-year separation process from EDC. Jon traded his ownership share to his brother Bill, in exchange for his personal ownership of Glastender. This venture came with a high degree of risk, but it was a risk Jon felt compelled to take.

Jon had this to say about his decision to phase out of the more secure EDC and start his own enterprise: "With my passion for designing and building things, I saw a greater future for me, my family, our employees, and our customers through selling things we manufacture, rather than through selling other people's products, as was the case with EDC. I knew that I had to build the capacity to do that because when I was selling other people's products, I kept running out of customers to buy what I was selling at the time."

Through this five year process, Jon remained responsible for the administration and oversight of EDC's finances. Jon remembers this as a time of great fear and uncertainty. It was a sink-or-swim time for Glastender.

On his way to success, Jon took the proverbial road less traveled: He dropped out of high school after completing the tenth grade and enrolled in night school classes at Saginaw High School. Then, when he lost his driver's license because he had accumulated multiple speeding tickets, he enlisted with Uncle Sam to serve in the U.S. Army, wherein on the ship, he committed to becoming a better version of himself. After he was honorably discharged from the military, he met, romanced, and married Brenda Keiser, the love of his life. Together for over 55 years, they have raised five children.

Quite remarkably, Glastender survived and grew from the mid-eighties on, in the midwest area that was increasingly being labeled as part of the manufacturing "rust belt." Many manufacturing plants were closing or moving overseas.

Jon's unique business success during this time can be attributed to his core belief that manufacturing is the heart and soul of America's free enterprise system. He also believes that profit is patriotic.

Generating profits for Jon is simply a measure of one's success in providing excellent products and services, and giving back to the community. To Jon, profit is essential to success in business, but profitability alone is not the goal. To meet and exceed the expectations of customers, shareholders, and employees is the real goal. To do this requires a fearless commitment to:

- manufacturing quality products.
- being best or first to market.
- being truly customer- and supplier-focused.
- being willing and able to prepare and bring offspring into the business with no sense of entitlement.
- being committed to building a culture that embraces employees as extended family.
- being profitable enough to become a generative contributor to the community through a variety of philanthropic endeavors.

The company's product portfolio includes glass washers, cocktail stations, modular bar die, underbar and back bar coolers, slide top coolers, mug frosters, beer dispensing systems, food equipment, and bottle disintegration systems. Newly introduced is commercial kitchen equipment.

Woven throughout Jon's story is the unmistakable contribution of mentors in his life. He turned to others to get what he needed to fulfill his purpose. Jon believes no one ever makes it alone! He fearlessly engaged people who could teach, nurture, and mentor him in ways that enabled him to do things on his own. As he says, "I wanted to learn from experts who could help me learn to build and fix things myself. I had lots of support. I was good at finding mentors. Everything I built, both then and now, was focused on reason and on improving functionality, safety, and attractiveness. I always needed to know the *why* behind all that I do. I will be forever grateful to those who helped me. Everything I learned from others, I saw as a means to get somewhere."

Jon Hall
Hicks Studio

As Paul Harvey, radio broadcaster for the ABC Radio Networks would say, "And now, the rest of the story!"

Chapter Two

ALONG CAME JON

W illiam Henry Hall married Veronica Elizabeth Boland at St. Andrew Church in Saginaw, Michigan, in 1927. They were both 26 years old. He was an ambitious entrepreneur and she was a very petite and proper homemaker who stood only five feet tall and weighed one hundred and eight pounds. She liked to dress to the nines and William loved to indulge her with nice clothes. She was no Imelda Marcos, who left behind at least 1,220 pairs of shoes when she died, but she did have a passion for fancy footwear. This couple truly enjoyed each other's company as they raised their three children.

Their first child, William Jr., was born in 1932. He was born prematurely so he needed extra care. He was a compliant child who generally followed the rules and manifested an easy-going personality. Five years later, daughter Veronica was born. She was their princess, raised as a little lady with ribbons in her hair, cute girly dresses, and the manners of a charm school graduate.

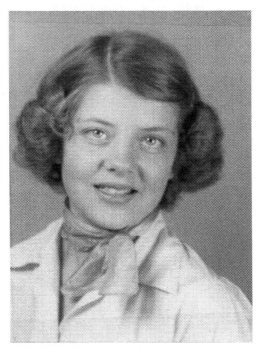

Veronica Hall, age thirteen

Three years later, on March 19, 1940 — along came Jon.

Jon's mother was 39 years old at the time of his birth. Veronica said, "My brothers, Bill and Jon, were completely different souls. Little Jon was much more independent and difficult for Mom and Dad to understand or handle. He was extremely inquisitive, very active, and would focus intently on what he was interested in, blocking out potential distractions. He was much less social than the rest of us, preferring to play by himself."

Jon showed an early desire to build things and would entertain himself for hours. For example, his father bought him an American Flyer electric train set when he was eight years old. As Jon put it, "Dad bought me the American Flier set because he thought it was more realistic, having two tracks versus the three-track Lionel train sets that most of my friends had. I enjoyed adding more cars, tracks, and other accessories until the basement floor was a miniature railroad station."

Jon, on right, age three

Don Wynn knew Jon as a child. His father worked for Jon's father, Bill, and was a close family friend. Don sometimes spent time watching over Jon when their parents were busy with other things. Don went on to help take Glastender nationally by becoming its first national sales representative. Jon literally put him in a motor home with a glass washer to introduce Glastender products to the rest of the country. Eventually a national network of sales representatives was established, with Don becoming the representative for the state of Ohio.

Lifelong friendship and business relationship
between Don Wynn, age 89, and Jon Hall

According to Don Wynn, "As a child, Jon was a loner, pretty self-centered, and kind of rowdy. He mostly played with his trains and things by himself. He found ways to add additional tracks, cars, and other accessories that really embellished his play." Jon appears to agree with Wynn as he remembers, "I spent most of my time by myself." Jon eventually sold the complete American Flyer train set to Butch's Pawn Shop, located on Hamilton Street on Saginaw's west side. Even at an early age, Jon was thinking about the next best thing and how to fund it.

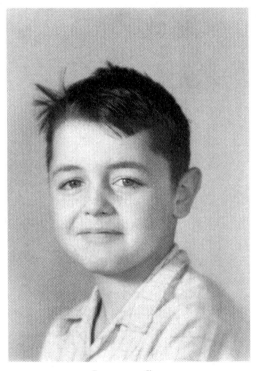

Jon, age five

The following stories manifest Jon's penchant for adventure. One time Grandpa Boland found him tightrope walking the railing of his home's second floor balcony. Jon's wife, Brenda, remembers his mother stating, "This was the only time I ever heard my father swear." When Jon was around age five, the police brought him home when they found him alone in the middle of the Court Street Bridge. After this happened, Jon's mom put him in a harness on a dog run when he was playing outside. Another time, Jon broke up a marble table and buried it in the backyard, explaining later to his unhappy mother that he was simply burying a treasure.

Elementary school was a challenge for Jon and his teachers. He showed little interest in what was being taught and the Sisters of Mercy who taught at St. Andrew Elementary School were not prepared to recognize, value, or nurture his unique artistic and design talents and interests.

* * *

This classic story about Thomas Edison might serve as an example of how teachers sometimes unwittingly underestimate the intelligence and motivations of children who might, in fact, be highly gifted:

One day, Thomas Edison came home and gave a folded-up paper to his mother. He said, "My teacher gave this paper to me and told me to only give it to my mother."

His mother's eyes were tearful as she read the letter out loud to her child: "Your son is a genius. This school is too small for him and doesn't have enough good teachers for training him. Please teach him yourself."

Many, many years after Edison's mother died and he was now one of the greatest inventors of the century, he discovered the truth about that note. One day as he was looking through old family documents, he saw a folded paper in the corner of a drawer. He opened it up and read:

> Your son is addled [mentally ill]. We won't let him come to school anymore."

Edison cried, then he wrote in his diary:

> Thomas Alva Edison was an addled child that, by a hero mother, became the genius of the century."

This story's authenticity is questioned by some. Whether it is literally true or not matters little. It makes a profound point about how children's motivations and intelligence can be overlooked or misunderstood by teachers.

* * *

It would be a mistake to assign too much blame to teachers in the 1950s who, lacking knowledge of multiple intelligences, may have underestimated the intelligence of some of the children in their care. It was three decades later before Harvard University professor Howard Gardner differentiated intelligence into seven specific *modalities*, rather than defining intelligence as dominated by a single general ability.

Gardner proposed his intelligence paradigm in his 1983 book, *Frames of Mind: The Theory of Multiple-Intelligences.* Gardner described seven modalities in his book:

1. Musical-rhythmic and harmonic: sensitivity to sounds, rhythms, tones, and music. People high in this intelligence have good pitch and can sing, play musical instruments, and compose music.
2. Visual-spatial: the ability to visualize with the mind's eye.

3. Verbal-linguistic: a facility with words and language. Typically, good at reading, writing, telling stories, and memorizing.
4. Logical-mathematical: A facility that has to do with logic, abstractions, reasoning, numbers, and critical thinking (this is closely linked to general intelligence).
5. Bodily-kinesthetic: control of one's bodily motions and the capacity to handle objects skillfully.
6. Interpersonal: sensitivity to other people's moods, feelings, temperaments, motivations, and their ability to cooperate and work as part of a team or group.
7. Intrapersonal: introspective and self-reflective capacities.

In 1995, Gardner identified an eighth intelligence – Naturalistic: the ability to make consequential distinctions in the world and use this ability productively (as hunters, gatherers, and farmers).

The faculty at St. Andrew Elementary School addressed a strong basic education with a focus on the verbal-linguistic and logical-mathematical intelligences and religion. The intelligences later defined by Gardner, and manifested by Jon and others with special interests and talents, were not realized at this time.

Having consulted with a multitude of private and public schools, my observation is that, sadly, despite Gardner's breakthrough research, this basic educational approach remains the focus in most public and private schools in America today. In practice, there appears to be an ever-narrowing focus on teaching and testing verbal-linguistic and logical-mathematical competencies at the expense of subjects such as art, music, physical education, and vocational education. Performing arts schools and vocational schools have nearly disappeared but the need for them is perhaps stronger than ever. Charter schools have been attempting to fill that void.

Though not recognized by the school system, Jon was clearly gifted in what Gardner calls the visual-spatial domain. In the social-emotional domains — not so much.

Jon's daughter, Kim, speaks to her father's unique intelligence when she says, "Dad is obviously very intelligent and has an amazing ability to design and build, but his emotional and social intelligence does lag behind. For example, he will sometimes say something to someone that offends them, and he doesn't even recognize that it does. Once, many years ago, he told my overweight brother-in-law we were dining with, 'You need to get better at pushing yourself away from the table.' He did not see that as offensive, although it was." Gardner would say that Jon may be somewhat lacking in the interpersonal intelligence domain.

While the school setting was not meeting Jon's needs, there were mentors outside of school who were nurturing his creative and artistic talents. Dad, Grandpa Boland, and Uncle Frank Ueltschi were early influences.

Jon's father, William, clearly served as a mentor. He exposed Jon to the business world and was a living example of the entrepreneurial spirit that drives the American free enterprise system.

According to Jon, "Dad was always working. He was one of the original sixteen distributors of Minute Maid and Honor Brand Frozen Foods products. These companies existed before Birdseye, Inc. He also owned and operated a chicken processing plant."

While recognizing his dad's ambition and entrepreneurship, Jon observed some traits that he did not want to emulate. "Dad was always light-years ahead of what customers wanted and generally charged too little for his products and services. For example, he would sell freezers filled with frozen foods, while making no profits on the freezers that he had financed through the bank. He simply hoped that once people had freezers, they would want to buy more Minute Maid and Honor Brand products. He didn't add profit margin to the freezers because he thought the banks might object. He clearly didn't understand how banks really work."

Jon adds, "While Dad did have some business shortcomings, he was willing to take risks. For example, he borrowed the money necessary to have Draper Chevrolet build refrigerated trucks for his business. He was the first in the area to do so. He also bought a 120-acre farm in Alma, Michigan that he had his brother-in-law operate. It was an old duck farm that he had plowed over so he could grow his own produce."

Veronica and William Hall on their 50th wedding anniversary, 1977

Jon's father and mother enjoyed spending time together but showed sparse interest in what Jon was doing. According to Jon, "Mom and Dad didn't pay much attention to what I was doing." Again, this was the typical parenting style back then.

It seems important to note here that prior to Dr. Spock and the onset of the baby boom generation that was born after 1946, parents would not focus on the arrangement of playdates and other diversions. They focused on the production of a miniature grown-up, conformed to adult notions of virtue and industry, ready for near-immediate employment. Jon tagged along with his father and was expected to help out with whatever had to be done. Like factory workers, children were not indulged, they were to be managed. Until the mid-1940s, children were to be formed according to their parents' wishes and society's needs, with parenting a matter of coercing useful behaviors, instead of catering to children's whims.

Dr. Benjamin Spock changed things in an instant. With the assistance of his wife, he produced *The Commonsense Book of Baby and Child Care*, first published in 1946, in time to guide Boomer upbringings. A best seller of tremendous proportions, it sold 500,000 copies in its first six months, and in the half-century following its printing, was surpassed only by the Bible in sales. Jon and his contemporaries were not beneficiaries of Spock's parental advice.

His other two early role models poured attention on Jon. According to Jon's sister, Veronica, "Grandpa Boland patiently showed Jon how to use and care for his tools. I recall watching them create things together on Grandpa's work bench. Grandpa was from Germany. He visited the United States when he was 14 years old and chose to return as an adult. Unfortunately, Grandpa Boland died when Jon was only seven years old."

Uncle Frank was a lifelong mentor to Jon. He played a significant role in modeling and coaching the creative thought processes and behaviors that proved to play a key role in molding and shaping Jon's talents. He was a living example of philosopher Plutarch's age-old advice: "Children are not vessels to be filled, they are fires to be lit."

Lifelong friend Arne Walli, Jon, and Uncle Frank

Veronica spoke fondly of Uncle Frank. "Uncle Frank was an artist. He would let Jon observe what he was doing, engaging Jon as he went along. Jon began to recognize and develop his own artistic and creative talents. In the Sears store entryway, Uncle Frank's painting of *Downtown*

Saginaw was displayed for all to see. That slightly-damaged painting is now a part of the city of Saginaw's Castle Museum's art collection. He also made puppets, similar to Howdy Doody. He would put on little puppet shows for Jon and me. The puppets would run up and down our arms. He also constructed little moving, mechanized characters that looked like they were scooping ice cream. These little characters were displayed in the malt shops that were popular at the time."

Jon reflects, "Uncle Frank once made a truck body out of a 1936 Chevy sedan. I was really impressed. He got me into wanting to creatively modify my bicycles and cars. He inspired me to observe how things worked and to come up with improvements in form, function, or both. I remember that one of my household chores was to empty the waste baskets into the furnace downstairs. I wanted to invent some way to make a chute, so I could empty the baskets directly into the furnace from upstairs. I never did accomplish that, but it was that kind of thinking that Uncle Frank's influence embedded in my thought processes."

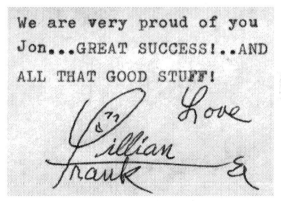

We are very proud of you Jon...GREAT SUCCESS!..AND ALL THAT GOOD STUFF!

Note from Uncle Frank to Jon

To shed more light on Jon's elementary and middle school years, I gathered some of his elementary, middle, and high school classmates from St. Andrew School to get some reflections on their memories of Jon as a classmate and as a student. Karen Bishop (Luplow), Barb LeFlair (Roeser), Janet Jacqmain (Jungerheld), Tom Polzin, Marc Matthews, and Mary Jo Neering (MacPhail) were among those who shared memories. Mary Jo laughingly shares, "I had a big crush on Jon in the seventh grade, but I don't think he knew I existed." There was a consensus that Jon was good looking, a quiet loner, and a person of few words in school.

Jon and I (Don Steele) would walk to school together on occasion and we played on the same elementary school basketball team. I always liked Jon and couldn't quite figure out why he wasn't more interested in sports. I believe that he could have excelled if he had shown any real interest. While our careers took us in different directions, we have remained lifelong friends.

Jon's closest friends during his elementary and middle school years were Marc Matthews, Paul Rummler (deceased), Jim Kirshner (deceased), and Tom Polzin.

Marc Matthews offered the following observations:

> I always admired Jon's creativity with his bicycles and cars. When he said he was going to do something, he did it. For a while, we tried to look as if we were rebels like James Dean or Marlon Brando in the movies. Some nights, we would drive cars off a car lot when the keys had been left in the ignition. These exciting adventures abruptly came to an end after Officer Ed Sproll came to my house to question me about a stolen tractor. Fortunately, we were not involved with that. Apparently, however, the police were somewhat aware of our antics. That marked the end of our joy rides."

Tom Polzin offered this insightful description:

> I first got to know Jon in middle school at St. Andrew. Inner-looking, very quiet, standing taller than his peers in his hip-hanging jeans and a swept-back D.A. haircut, Jon Hall was considered by some to be a tough guy and a renegade — unless they talked with him. Soft dark eyes of kindness, hurt, and determination belied his demeanor. Jon had swagger and sex appeal

and could handle himself in a fight if he needed to, but what he sought most was trust, friendship, and recognition. He gave it in return but found little in his school years.

"In many ways, he was alone to himself, finding it difficult to find others who were interested in what interested him, which was building things. He and I operated in different circles after class, but I always found him easy to talk to. He was genuine, with a vulnerable honesty, under a subterfuge of roughness. He couldn't hide it then, and he still can't now.

"I visited Glastender on business in 1988 (he happened to have been away) so I was aware of his success, but sixty years passed since school before I saw him again. I had left for ten years in the Catholic seminary after the eighth grade, and he had left school after the tenth grade to pursue a lifetime of creativity in the business world. Whereas I was an academic, he was more driven to action and decision: a difference between us that was never a barrier, but rather a valence of opposites, a curiosity and a liking that pertained decades later.

"Sixty years — then twice in the last four years. The first of two conversations were with both Jon and his most gracious wife, Brenda, after mass in 2013. He didn't recognize me at first, but that is my point here. Guarded for a moment, he was open, considerate, and enthusiastic — no matter whom I might be. Nonetheless, with just a few keys to the past, the connection came of age, and we were classmates once again."

It was in those middle school years that Jon's creative design talents began to really blossom. Jon's father may have contributed to this growth by always choosing to buy Jon unique gifts that featured special qualities and/or creativity. For example, when he bought Jon his first bicycle, it was a Columbia. Jon had wanted a Schwinn, but his father bought him a Columbia because it had a front spring fork that served as a shock-absorber. Not easily influenced when it came to design, Jon quickly modified his bike by removing the sprung front fork and replacing the handlebars with a steering wheel.

When Jon discovered that Saginaw's Montgomery Ward Department Store was sponsoring a yearly bicycle parade that offered the possibility of winning a new bicycle, he sprang into action. For his first entry, he didn't know that he was supposed to decorate his bike featuring a safety slogan. He had made his first entry look like an elephant. The body, trunk and all, were made of cardboard and painted gray. Jon embossed the name *Elmer* on it. Unfortunately, because his entry lacked a required safety slogan, he didn't win a prize. His entry was so unique and creative, however, that *Elmer* was the featured picture in the *Saginaw News* story about the contest. Jon reflects, "Mom and Dad didn't even know I was doing this stuff." Once again, no applause.

For the next year's competition, Jon dressed up like an onion and, behind the seat of his bicycle, he created what looked like a petunia patch, adorned with flowers. This time he had safety slogans: *Don't be an onion in a petunia patch. Play it safe!* Jon won third place. Still, no applause.

The third year, Jon captured the top prize by creating a merry-go-round on his bike that featured four horses, each adorned with a safety slogan, such as: *Mary goes around safely, why don't you?* And *Don't horse around, play it safe.* Jon's first place prize won him a brand-new English Racer bicycle. He was just 14 years old at the time.

Instead of doing what most kids would do, young entrepreneur Jon immediately sold his English Racer bicycle to a trick shop for $45. He used that money to purchase a used Whizzer motor bike that cost him $65. The other $20 came from money Jon had saved from his earnings shoveling snow in the winter and from selling ice cream bars (at two cents profit per bar) in the summer.

The Whizzer didn't run well, so he sought help from the mechanics at Pretzer's Garage. In addition to physical help with fixing his bike, Jon found mentors at Pretzer's Garage. Harold and Lowell Pretzer were mechanics who also did body and paint work on cars. Jon started hanging out at Pretzer's to watch them work on cars. He was 15 years old and eager to learn all he could about cars. Both Harold and Lowell became friends and mentors to Jon.

According to Jon, "These guys were always willing to take the time to teach me, as well as help me work on my own cars at no expense." Once he got it running well and looking good, he sold the Whizzer to the owner of Knutson's bicycle shop (later called Wesley's Bike Shop). He recovered his investment when he got $65 for it.

Jon's work on the Whizzer motorbike at Pretzer's Garage led to him getting a job sanding cars to get them ready for painting. He also had part-time jobs unloading trucks at night at Reliable Linen and delivering newspapers at 5:30 each morning. Reliable Linen had two employees that worked 3–6 p.m. They quit, Jon was hired in, and did all the work of the previous two employees. He made 80 cents per hour. The owner wouldn't give him a raise, even though Jon had saved him money, so he left and went to Saginaw Publishing Company, stocking and doing inventory.

Now it's clear why Jon didn't participate in sports! He was otherwise occupied with his passionate pursuit of earning money to support his creative design ambitions.

One might read into Jon's elementary and high school background that he was a bit of an outcast; actually, he was very well-liked and was not ostracized by his teachers or his classmates. He was simply very purposeful in his quest to know how to design and build things — interests not shared by most of his teachers and classmates. With the need to earn money to support his endeavors, he had little time or interest in what the school had to offer or in chumming around with people who didn't share his purpose or passion. I am rather sure that people like Bill Gates and Steve Jobs fit a similar profile.

Jon is much better described by the term "outlier," as defined by Malcomb Gladwell in his book of the same name. Gladwell defines an outlier as a person out of the ordinary who doesn't fit the normal understanding of achievement. He says, "Great men and women are beneficiaries of specialization, collaboration, time, space, and culture. An outlier's recipe for success is not personal mythos but the synthesis of opportunity and time on task."

Gladwell attempts to answer the question, "What makes some

people successful while others cannot seem to realize their potential?" Gladwell claims that Mozart and the Beatles are not so much innate musical prodigies but grinders who thrived only after 10,000 hours of practice. Jon clearly meets and surpasses that standard. In school, Jon was an outlier in a world of sameness. Memorizing and conforming, qualities prized in school, were of little interest to Jon. As he moved into the upper grades, Jon began to find opportunities to achieve in areas of importance to himself, even if conventional thinking of the time didn't recognize it.

Chapter Three

JON'S HIGH SCHOOL YEARS

D uring his high school years, Jon was not close to his siblings Bill or Veronica. This lack of camaraderie was primarily due to their age differences and the changing cultural beliefs, attitudes, behaviors, and dress codes of those years. Bill and Veronica were more representative of the earlier generation while Jon and his peers were on the cusp of introduction to rock and roll music, duck-tail hair styles, hot rods, and casual dress. Elvis Presley, Little Richard, Chuck Berry, Jerry Lee Lewis, and the like were all the rage, and being hip meant being, or at least appearing to be, rebellious (a not-too-uncommon goal for teenagers of any generation).

Jon entered his freshman year of high school at St. Andrew in 1955, an eventful time in the dramatically-changing culture and mores of America. To list just a few facts:

- The movie *Rebel Without a Cause* was a smash hit with teenagers.
- Rosa Parks was arrested for refusing, as a black woman, to go to the back of the bus.
- Rock and roll music's popularity surged, featuring emerging and controversial stars such as Elvis Presley, Bill Haley and the Comets, and Chuck Berry and the Platters.
- Seat belts were mandated on all new cars.

- The first McDonald's fast food restaurant was erected, and TV dinners appeared.
- The first cans of Coca-Cola were sold (until then, this soft drink had only been sold in bottles).
- Jonas Salk's polio vaccine was declared safe and effective. The Mickey Mouse Club debuted.
- The United States began its involvement in the Vietnam conflict.
- Clothing fashions for teens changed, modeled after James Dean and others (pink and black were wildly-fashionable clothing and shoe colors).

St. Andrew School was a Roman Catholic private school where Jon and I were classmates. Much like the elementary and middle school years, Sisters of Mercy nuns (a possible oxymoron) taught a social and economic cross-section of students from Saginaw, Carrollton, Zilwaukee, Shields, and other surrounding communities. The focus of the curriculum was on college prep and the religious doctrines of the Roman Catholic faith. Acceptance, success, and popularity were achieved primarily through sports or academic achievement. Girls were deprived of the opportunity to participate in sports. There were little or no vocational or artistic curricular choices that matched up well with Jon's talents or interests.

Jon, age fifteen

Jon sported a flat-top haircut, duck-tailed, Elvis-style, and favored wearing jeans and a tee shirt (this has not changed). While he was athletically built, he chose work over sports. He quit playing football after his eighth-grade year because he was offered a job at a gas station that paid five dollars per day. That wage would enable him to spend more time on his projects. He told me, "Wherever work was, I made money at it!"

Jon struggled academically in high school. A significant finding sheds some light on a specific trait that Jon clearly exemplified. Tom Corley, an accountant and financial planner, surveyed several high-net-worth individuals, many of whom are self-made millionaires. He found that most of the people he surveyed did not earn high GPAs (Grade Point Averages) in high school. In fact, 21% of the self-made millionaires were A students. 41% were B students and 29% were C students. That's right: More of the self-made millionaires were C students than were A students. If you are wondering if family background played a part, 59% of the self-made millionaires came from middle class homes and 41% came from poor households — proving where you start does not dictate where you finish.

As Corley writes, "… success in life does not come easy. It is fraught with pitfalls, obstacles, failure, and mistakes. Success requires persistence, along with mental and emotional toughness in overcoming these pitfalls. Its pursuit pushes you to the edge emotionally and physically. We must grow a thick skin and become accustomed to struggle if we hope to succeed. Individuals who struggle academically may be more accustomed to dealing with struggle and making it a daily habit to overcome pitfalls." In short, people like Jon Hall become mentally tough, which creates a foundation for long-term success.

Successful people are great at delaying gratification and withstanding temptation. They are also willing and able to overcome fear and do what they need to do. Successful people, like Jon, don't just prioritize. They consistently keep doing what they have decided is important.

Jon dropped out of St. Andrew after he completed the tenth grade. After returning from the service, he attended night school at Saginaw High School where he could take classes that more closely aligned with his interests. He eventually earned the credits necessary to be awarded his diploma from St. Andrew High School.

Jon obviously didn't let grades in school define him. He manifests the fact that the past doesn't define you. The past is just training. When it comes down to it, "school" is never over. Successful people, like Jon, are lifelong learners.

All too often, IQ is used as a measure of likely-success in school and in life. Recent research reveals, however, that a person's IQ can change over time. It's not fixed. Because you were a C student at 17 with an IQ of 100 doesn't necessarily mean that you stay that way. You can increase (or decrease) your IQ all during your life, even into your 80s. Self-made millionaires do certain things daily that improve their brains and continuously increase their intelligence during their lifetimes. Malcom Gladwell, in his book *Outliers,* presents strong evidence to support the fact that mastery of any complex task, from learning to play violin to becoming a master criminal, requires 10,000 hours of disciplined practice. Simply stated, innate ability is never enough.

Angela Duckworth, a psychologist at the University of Pennsylvania, is the foremost researcher on grit and self-control and the founder and CEO of Character Lab. Her passion is to advance the service and practice of character development through the Lab.

Characteristics of grit, as defined by Angela, are:

- Courage
- Conscientiousness
- Long-term goals
- Resilience
- Excellence vs. perfection

In her book, *Grit,* Angela explains that "grit is the driver of achievement of success. Without grit, talent may be nothing more than unmet potential. It is only with effort that talent becomes a skill that leads to success."

Jon's continuous learning is exemplified by his shift in interest from bicycles to learning about cars as he became a teen. Even though he was too young to drive, he used the $68.72 he had saved to buy his first car, a 1937 Chevy two-door sedan. Being fifteen at the time, Jon could only drive his car up and down the driveway. Just two weeks later, he traded it even-up for a 1936 four-door Cadillac that a guy sold to him because it was too big for his wife to drive.

The seller originally wanted $100 for his Cadillac, but Jon told him he had the perfect car for his wife to drive. The seller agreed to an even exchange once he saw Jon's Chevy. Two weeks later, the seller wanted his car back. Jon's dad, backing up Jon, said, "You made a deal, stick with it!" I trust that Dad's response felt like applause to Jon.

Fellow student Jim Fiebig (now Jim Berlin) shares this story: "A bunch of us guys from St. Andrew went to Winona Beach Amusement Park. Jon was driving his 1936 Cadillac with a big stick shift mounted on the floor. He let me drive. I had never driven before, and my left leg was shaking as I engaged the clutch and ground the gears. Jon said, 'Don't worry, you can't hurt this thing.'"

Through the ages of 16 and 17, Jon bought, modified, and sold a lot of cars. He traded the 1936 Cadillac for a 1941 Chevy that he painted at Pretzer's Garage using leftover paint he mixed into a color he liked. He would get the materials and tools he needed to sand and paint his cars in exchange for doing odd jobs for the Pretzer's Garage guys. Jon traded the 1941 Chevy for a 1929 Ford panel truck. He painted it red with green fenders. Then, he traded the 1929 panel truck to Wimpy's Junk Yard for a 1931 Model A Coupe.

Jon's 1947 Ford Coupe

During this time, Jon grew four or five inches in height, causing him to be too tall to drive his 1931 Model A, so he traded it for a 1947 Ford Coupe that he painted sandstone beige. He removed the door handles and he removed the chrome. He then traded that car for a customized 1949 chop-topped Ford.

At the age of 17, Jon spent a year working in construction. He built houses off of Hess Street in Saginaw. According to Jon, he would rough the houses in, then come back later to install windows and flooring.

This period in Jon's life, with its unique combination of mentors, ambition, culture change, personal idiosyncrasies, events, and circumstances, appears to have converged to mold and shape Jon's creative and artistic skills in ways that would prove to serve him very well in his adult entrepreneurial pursuits. His focus, creativity, work ethic, and money management skills served as the foundation for the business success he would eventually come to enjoy in founding and operating his now second-generation, family-owned and -operated business enterprise. The trajectory of his life, however, was about to change in a very good way — because of one thing: speeding tickets. The loss of his driver's license caused Jon to answer Uncle Sam's call to action, "We need you!"

Chapter Four

HE'S IN THE ARMY NOW!

G athering speeding tickets while driving his hot rod cars and
lacking a "Get Out of Jail Free" card, Jon decided to enlist
in Uncle Sam's army. To Jon, losing his driver's license was
akin to the Lone Ranger having his horse, Silver, taken away. Jon says,
"I decided to join the service because, if I couldn't drive, what's the
purpose of remaining in Saginaw?"

He was 18 years old, and the year was 1958. Perhaps the best thing
about joining the army at that time was the fact that he got to choose
his job. Considering all the possibilities, Jon picked working on missiles.

One important goal Jon set for himself when he enlisted was to get to Germany. Germany was Grandpa Boland's homeland prior to his moving to the United States and Jon had heard many stories about it.

Jon's mother offered surprising advice as he left for the service of his country, stating, "Sew your wild oats while you are in Germany!" He would have to wait a while before he could get to Germany (or act on mom's advice) because his first stop would be in nearby Romulus, Michigan. He was stationed at Detroit Metro Airport where he would work with others in assembling missiles in a secret underground area located under the airport.

At the time Jon joined the army, three Nike missile sites were based in Downriver Detroit. Jon was stationed at D-61, the last site to open and the last site to be shut down by the U.S. Military. These missile sites were of vital importance to our nation's defense.

From January 1955 to February 1963, Detroit was provided protection from post-World War II attack. This was part of a complicated and detailed protection plan spanning the area between Detroit and Cleveland. Each facility was fully equipped with numerous Nike Ajax and eventually Nike Hercules missiles ready at a moment's notice should post-war conditions warrant an attack.

The reasons behind the military protection of Detroit at the time were numerous and understandable. During World War II, the city had earned the title "Arsenal of Democracy" because it was among the nation's leaders in wartime production of weaponry and military transportation. Also taken into consideration was Detroit's long-standing ties with Canada, which had long wanted to avoid war. The third and most obvious reason may have been the city's continued standing as the automotive capital of the world.

The Detroit facility where Jon was stationed began operations in June of 1957 and was commanded by the 594th U.S. Battalion, Battery C. The location was near the present-day intersection of Middlebelt and Goddard Roads, to the west side. The launch facility where Jon worked was located on the airport property. In the late 1950s, the operation was taken over by the 177th Michigan Army National Guard (MIARNG). This site would be active later than the others and would be the only one of the three Downriver sites to make the transition from Nike Ajax to the further redeveloped Hercules series. Jon participated in this transition.

The Nike Hercules (initially designated as SAM-A-25, and later, MIM-14) was a surface-to-air missile used by U.S. and NATO armed forces for medium- and high-altitude long-range air defense. It was normally armed with the W31 nuclear warhead but could also be fitted with a conventional warhead for export use. The Hercules was developed as the successor to the earlier Nike Ajax.

Jon worked on both the Nike Hercules and the Nike Ajax missile projects. He says, "The missiles we assembled were all new and they rested on launchers. Our job was to assemble the missiles and make sure everything was in working order with the launching mechanisms before they were sent to Texas. When we transitioned to the larger Nike Hercules, each missile took four Ajax boosters and was armed with a nuclear warhead that was bigger than the bombs we dropped on Japan."

The next mentor to Jon came during this period of joining the U.S. Army. Master Sergeant Moore was the head of Ajax Missile assembly. He challenged Jon to create an inventory system for the parts used in missile production. The parts were scattered around with no identification, so Jon ordered one of every part in order to find out their part numbers. Then he created a new supply system that ensured tracking and timely restocking of the parts. He also taught Jon to never accept "No," and how to work around, through, or over people to get things done. Jon stated, "Moore could yell so loud your pants would fall off. He was scary, as most master sergeants would be. However, he and I had a good working relationship, especially after I completed the project."

Jon, age 21

Jon spent a little less than a year at the base in Romulus, and then sailed, along with 300 other soldiers, to Europe. On his way overseas, Jon made a profound personal commitment that would shape his life from that day forward. Jon made this one-time affirmation:

> " I will do the best I can, in all things, while serving in Germany and afterwards."

This was a decision of the heart rather than a decision of the mind. Decisions such as what we will wear on a given day or what movie we are going to go see are decisions of the mind. Decisions of the heart are life-changing affirmations that make us into better people. From that day forward, Jon metaphorically became like one of the Nike heat-seeking missiles that he had worked on. These missiles *track their target until they score a hit.* In Jon's professional life, like the surface-to-air missiles, Jon stays focused on what is most important to him and readily adapts to targets that can be very elusive.

For example, Jon says, "My first commitment to doing the best I could was to learn the German language. However, when I requested lessons in the German language, I was told that I lacked the army's one year of college prerequisite. Rather than give up on my commitment, I continued to pursue my target along another pathway. To meet my commitment, I negotiated an arrangement whereby I would teach English in exchange for getting lessons in the German language. It worked. I learned enough German to get by."

Jon adds, "On the voyage from the United States to Europe, we spent one day in London before deploying to Germany and taking up residence at the Kelly Barracks in Darmstadt. Unlike the Romulus location that only housed twelve people in the barracks, Kelly Barracks had several buildings full of soldiers. My job was to take care of all the secret materials to ensure that if we were the first battery to go operational in Europe, everything would be in order. By the way, while we were telling everyone in Germany that we had no nuclear warheads, I was right there working on them."

Jon further explained, "The top brass from Washington would do periodic checks to make sure things were being done right. In most cases, the higher the level of command that did the inspection, the less comprehensive the inspection was. That was not the case with us. In fact, when it came to missile inspection, it was very much the opposite. Inspections were thorough, and security was tight. We had double barbed wire fences and 50-caliber machine guns stationed at the corners of the property to ensure our security."

Jon was assigned an army-issued jeep that he got to use as part of his assembly job in Germany. Jon, being Jon, painted it and put yellow terry cloth seat covers on it to spiff it up. It really stood out from the rest of the jeeps on the base.

One day a friend of his drove up next to Jon's jeep with a captain as his passenger. As Jon tells us, "The two of them walked around my jeep several times, all the while talking about how neat it was. Then, out of the blue, the captain says to his driver, 'See our new jeep!' Off they went in my jeep."

Jon replaced his jeep with this Volkswagen Bug

Jon quickly bought a 1951 Volkswagen Bug to replace his jeep. He paid for it with his own money so there was no chance he would have to surrender it to someone higher up in the military pecking order. He called his dad, asking him to send some Bondo so he could fix up the body of his VW. "I went into our warhead facility and used two separate trucks, one to provide the air and another to provide the lighting to shine the lights on the car at night so I could see enough to sand and paint it. I got the paint from the Air Force, so, of course, it was blue. I made cut-outs in the back bumper and installed a dual exhaust system like the ones on the newer VW models."

During this time, Jon enjoyed a special friendship with a German chess master who taught him the game. This chess master was so good that he could play five people at a time and beat them all. He invited Jon to join his chess team and they competed in competitions all over Germany. Jon relates, "I was the fifth man on the team, but what I learned from these competitions about thinking strategically was really beneficial in life and in my career."

Jon had not taken a leave in two years, so he was granted a 21-day leave. He decided to take a trip through Italy. He agreed to take a friend along because his friend told him he could speak Italian. Jon learned, too late, that his friend had lied about that.

Before leaving for Italy with his friend, Jon took a solo trip to the General Walker Hotel in Obersalzberg, Germany, where he participated in a Catholic religious retreat. The General Walker Hotel was the former Pension Moritz Boarding House and boasted opulent accommodations and sweeping views of the Bavarian countryside and Alpine scenery. It opened in 1878 and was renamed Platterhof in 1928. After the Nazi seizure of power, it became part of the extended containment area around Hitler's headquarters at the nearby Berghof residence, serving as a guest house and meeting facility of the SS guards. Following World War II, the damaged building was restored as a U.S. Armed Forces Recreation Center and again renamed after U.S. Army General Walton Walker (1889–1950). Walker was killed in the Korean War. In one of life's curious turns, twenty years after Jon's stay at the General Walker Hotel, he was back there again, trying to sell Glastender products to the U.S. Army. The complex was demolished in 2000.

Jon left Darmstadt with his friend and enjoyed a stay at the Garmisch Ski Resort and Spa, located about 60 miles from Munich, the 1936 Summer Olympics host. It was situated around Germany's highest mountain, Zugspitze, that straddles the Austrian border. Jon witnessed the beautiful Burches Gardens, a place he and his family would later visit and agree that it is one of the most beautiful places on earth.

Brenner Pass navigates through the Alps and forms the border between Italy and Austria. It is one of the principal passes of the Eastern Alpine range and has the lowest altitude among Alpine passes of the area. However, it was hazardous for Jon to drive, because the brakes on his VW were manual and it was all he could do to simply slow the car down on the steep grade. The fact that the car had no safety glass added to the excitement. Despite these challenges, Jon manage to safely maneuver his VW down through Brenner Pass into Italy.

Jon (seated second from right) with some friends in Italy

Traveling down the eastern coast of Italy, their first stop was Venice. From there, they went to Florence and then on to Rome, where they got to see Pope John XXIII offer Mass. In Rome, Jon visited with a school teacher he knew. He also visited with military friends stationed at a naval base in Naples.

Returning to Darmstadt, Jon completed his military commitment and was honorably discharged from the U.S. Army in May of 1961. He gave serious thought to staying in Germany, but his dad wanted him to come home. Jon joined his dad at EDC in 1961, eventually becoming a full partner in 1963.

After Jon came home from the military, he joined
his father at Equipment Distributing Co.

The first thing Jon did upon arrival in Saginaw was go to a couple of
Saginaw's landmark businesses. His first stop was at Tony's Restaurant
on Genesee Street where he indulged himself with its famous steak
sandwich. The next day, he went to Edward's Men Store to buy a suit.
He needed the suit for his first National Restaurant Association Trade
Show that was coming up — an event he would attend annually for the
next fifty years.

Jon enrolled in night classes at Saginaw High School and at Delta
College. He wanted to take solid geometry and trigonometry, classes
he felt would help him in business. Some classes he wanted to take were
not offered by Saginaw High School, so he asked the instructors if they
would offer those classes if he could gather enough interested students
to warrant adding them to their schedule. The staff agreed, and Jon
successfully recruited the necessary number of students to justify adding

these classes to the Saginaw High School night schedule. Jon also took classes in accounting and business law at Delta College because, "If I was going to own and run a business, I needed to know these things."

Jon's life-changing affirmation, "to do the best I can, in all things, while serving in Germany and afterwards," would serve Jon well as he moved forward with his family and business life.

A notable example of Jon's heat-seeking-missile capacity was made manifest when he met attractive young secretary Brenda Keiser.

Chapter Five

HERE COMES THE BRIDE!

I n 1963, when Jon returned from Germany, he met Brenda Keiser. Like the heat-seeking Nike Hercules missiles he had assembled in the military, Jon zeroed in on his target.

Only Jon knows if he followed his mom's advice and sowed his oats in Germany, but there is no question that he was more experienced in the ways of the world than Brenda. She had lived a rather sheltered life in northern Michigan. She was raised on Pleasant View Road between Mackinaw City and Cross Village and had graduated from high school one year early, at the tender age of 16, as salutatorian of her class! Brenda laughingly says, "I think Jon liked my innocence and the fact that I had a close-knit family. Looking back, I also believe he felt that, behind every successful man… there's a woman who will deliver a bunch of kids that will someday go to work for him." This gaze into her crystal ball proved to be very prophetic.

While Jon had been taking classes, working for his father's Equipment Distribution Company (EDC), and modifying his hot rods, Brenda had been studying at a business school in Grand Rapids.

At the age of 18, Brenda was introduced to Walter Averill by a friend who knew that Brenda liked doing secretarial work. Walter, the owner of Secretarial Services in Saginaw, hired her to help Mary Ellen Martin at their office, located on Michigan Avenue. Brenda remembers, "I was young, alone, and had no money. Walter and Mary Ellen really treated me well."

When Brenda moved to Saginaw for her job, she initially stayed at the Bancroft Hotel. After a month or so she moved into a small apartment above the Secretarial Service office. Then, in June of 1963, when Walter was appointed general chairman of Saginaw's Timber Town Festival Days, he asked Brenda to work at his Timber Town Headquarters in downtown Saginaw.

In July of 1963, a Ferris wheel was installed as a special attraction for the Timber Town Festival Days. Brenda recalls, "It was late afternoon and Walter had handed me a stuffed pink poodle. I carried it down to the street. Johnny Lee Fontaine, Marc Matthews, and Jon came walking by the Ferris wheel where I was standing. Jon stopped and asked me about the pink poodle I was holding. I told him that my boss had given it to me. Jon invited me to join him on a ride on the Ferris wheel. Walter Averill saw us and encouraged me to take him up on his offer. We exchanged basic info and after the guys left, I never gave it a second thought."

But Jon did.

Brenda recalls, "The next day was a Saturday. I went to a family wedding with my sister. On Sunday morning, I slept in until eleven o'clock in the morning. I was awakened by this loud knocking on my door. I didn't answer because I was in my pajamas. About noon, I decided to walk over to Anthony's Fine Foods, a nearby restaurant, for a late breakfast. As I was approaching Anthony's, I heard this loud car and someone yelling, 'Hello stuck-up!' It was Jon driving his El Camino. He invited himself to join me for breakfast. Over breakfast, Jon asked me if I wanted to see Bartell's garage where he was working on his original hot rod. It was painted a primer gray and was just a frame and body. Then, he invited me to go with him to a movie. I was kind of anxious because I hadn't dated a lot and I didn't know him well. I decided to go with him."

The El Camino Jon drove on his first date with Brenda, shown here on Ojibway Island, across from the Saginaw Waterworks

Brenda laughs as she says, "Every night for a month he was at my apartment. He was clearly more attentive in those days than he has been over the last fifty years of marriage."

Brenda adds, "We dated through August and I decided to take him up north to meet my family. We had a small home with no extra bedrooms, so I slept with my mother. My oldest sister invited Jon to sleep in their Airstream Travel Trailer, parked near the house. Jon says he nearly froze to death because it had no heat. He still talks about how cold he was that night.

"We were together constantly, but Jon was working a lot. Sometimes, I would ride with him as he made his service calls. It was early October before he took me to meet his mother at the house where Jon had been raised (808 Congress Street). I had already briefly met Jon's father. It was outside Naismith's Restaurant while I was accompanying Jon on one of his service calls. I found out later that it was Jon's mother, rather than Jon, who had invited me to join the family for dinner. I was introduced to a petite, attractive lady who cooked a great meal of prime rib and vegetables. I was the only one who ate everything, including the potato skins. I was a little embarrassed because when we ate at my home, everyone always ate the potato skins. After we were married, she told me she knew Jon was serious about me because he had never brought a girl home to meet his family before."

Brenda adds, "In November of 1963, Jon gave me an engagement ring. He proposed by setting a blue box with a ring in it on my desk at work. He is not really the romantic type but rather prefers the element of surprise. He looked at me with a big smile and waited for my reaction. We were married in Mackinaw City at St. Anthony Church by Fr. Linus Schrems on September 19, 1964."

Brenda was anxious to have children. They produced four children in four years: Jon Jr., Kimberly, Richard, and Todd. Thirteen years later, Brenda delivered their daughter, Kristina. Jon was able to invest more personal time in raising Kristina, taking her to school and spending time with her, things that he rarely, if ever, had time to do with the first four Hall offspring.

I asked Brenda to share a few observations about Jon. She mostly reaffirmed things discussed earlier when she said, "I think Jon didn't benefit much from school. The private school he attended drew people whose interests were different from Jon's. Jon wanted to design and build, and the curriculum did not address those interests."

Jon found a wonderful way to meet his need to build and to exercise his creativity outside of school. He vested his energies in modifying cars according to his own design. Recently, Jon purchased an El Camino truck resembling the one in which he picked Brenda up on their first dates. He completely restored it as a surprise for her on their 54ᵗʰ wedding anniversary.

Brenda and Jon
Hicks Studio

Brenda went on to say, "Jon can't be squeezed into someone else's mold. He loves his work, his kids, and his family. Jon never got the applause that people get from sports and other spectator endeavors. He generally worked alone, seldom stepping into any kind of spotlight. While his parents showed little interest in Jon's youthful activities, he proved to be a very good son, giving emotional and financial support to his parents during their later years."

Brenda focused her life on being a good wife and mother. She succeeded in both. Just as she was devoted to her children, she is now dedicated to her grandchildren. She never chose to engage in Jon's work. Her absence from that part of Jon's life led Jon's friend, Keith Crain, to jokingly suggest that he was keeping Brenda in a freezer in Mackinaw City.

The truth is, Brenda fully understood Jon's passion for his work and his commensurate workaholic schedule. Brenda recognized early that when Jon says, "I only work half-days — twelve hours a day," he is not kidding. Jon says, "I told Brenda, you take care of the kids for their first eighteen years, and I'll take over from there."

Brenda Hall is the unsung hero in Jon Hall's multi-generational, family-owned and -operated business success. She has chosen to apply her time and energy to the family side of the family-business equation.

Anyone who marries a workaholic like Jon needs to know that their husband will have a mistress that will occupy his thoughts and behaviors most of the time. Jon, in fact, has two mistresses. The first is his business. The second is his hot rods. Both take a lot of Jon's physical and emotional energy. This has left Brenda with a disproportionate share of family-related responsibilities that she accepts.

Does Jon love his Brenda? Yes. Brenda is his one and only love. Does he love his children? No doubt. His children mean the world to him. Is he a good provider? Yes. He and Brenda suffered through years of forced frugality while making things work on the home front as well as with the business. Is Jon the ideal husband? By some standards, the answer would be, "No." However, Brenda did not and does not feel that way. She "gets" Jon and accepts his passions for his work and his hot rods.

There is a frequently stated quote that says, "No one on their deathbed says, 'I wish I had spent more time at the office.'" This statement probably doesn't hold true for Jon. There are never enough hours in the day for him to fulfill his quest to perfect his Glastender products and build his better-than-factory-built hot rods.

Let's take a closer look.

First, Brenda had a pretty good idea of what she was getting into when she married Jon. She knew how dedicated he was to his work going into the marriage. Earlier I quoted Brenda when she said, "Looking back, I also believe that he felt that behind every successful man… there's a woman who will deliver a bunch of kids that will someday go to work for him." She knew that, for Jon, his dedication to his work wasn't about getting rich. It was more about fulfilling his commitment to doing the best he could in all things moving forward. She said, "I think it was Jon's military service experience that set him on the path to always doing the best he can do at whatever he takes on. He is also very honest. He learned from his dad, 'Never try to sell a customer a bill of goods.' When he came into his own, he was all in — 'I want to do this, I can do this, and I'm going to do well.'"

Brenda came from rather humble beginnings. Her father suffered from anxiety and depression issues that limited his ability to find and keep a good job. He also spent much time hospitalized, and therefore not at home. Her mom became the matriarch who looked after the well-being and education of their six children. She planted and harvested vegetables and canned everything possible for winter consumption. Mom clearly served as a role model for Brenda.

Like her mom, Brenda's personal wants and needs are few. She thinks more about the wants and needs of Jon and their children and of their grandchildren. To Brenda, family is everything. She has a very low tolerance for show-off behaviors. She has learned to really like hard rock music because her boys are engaged in it in a variety of ways. She attends basketball games, soccer games, and swim meets her grandkids participate in, often bringing Jon along.

I asked the Hall siblings to share some thoughts about their mom. Here are a few things they had to say:

- Mom allowed Dad to focus on his business and his hot rods.
- Mom showed great interest in all things we were involved in. She always had her trusty typewriter ready to go while prodding us to get our homework done.
- Mom learned to like our hard rock music and once even made a loin cloth for Jon Jr. when he was performing and paying tribute to his rock hero of the moment, Ted Nugent.
- Mom served as the disciplinarian.
- Mom is very affectionate — emotions running on 10. She manifests unconditional love.
- Mom can be our critic, but she won't let anyone else criticize us. She holds us accountable, but always does it one-on-one.
- Mom is close enough to perfect for us!

Brenda is the spirit of the family, breathing life into daily routines and special events.

Chapter Six

THE EQUIPMENT DISTRIBUTING COMPANY (EDC) YEARS

The year was 1954. One day, Jon's dad saw an ice machine, called a Clear Cube, and decided to sell those as a replacement for the small freezers that had ice cube trays he had been selling. He eventually shifted to renting them out to accommodate customers who wanted assurance that the service problems they were encountering would be handled as a part of the contract. The rental agreements included services for repair and replacement. Service was also available to those who purchased Clear Cube, but it came with an additional cost to those buyers.

Jon was about 14 when his dad asked him if he could fix broken ice machines. Jon became interested and started to learn what he needed to know about repairing the ice machines that were used at the time. Years later, while Jon was in Germany serving his country, he studied the Kold Draft ice machine manuals and became well-versed on how to repair their models also.

Upon discharge from the Army, Jon put this new knowledge to work as the service guy for his dad's Equipment Distributing Company (EDC). Dad had been sub-contracting a refrigeration technician to do the service work until Jon came on board. This responsibility kept Jon very busy because, over the next ten years, the rental business grew from 38 to over 500 ice machines covering Flint, Bay City, Saginaw, Midland, and the Lansing areas.

Unfortunately, according to Jon, "EDC never charged enough, so all we did was turn our receivables over to the bank to cover our financing. I believe that Dad was hoping the time would come when the ice machines would be paid for and he would realize a windfall of money. It never worked that way because by the time they were paid for, the customers needed new ones."

Jon explains, "Because Dad had lost income from most of his business ventures, he focused our efforts on the distribution of ice machines. Over a brief period of years, most of Dad's other businesses had dried up: Minute Maid dropped Dad as a sales rep and went to direct sales to the grocery stores. Honor Brand frozen foods disappeared because Birdseye started selling for less money, and others were underbidding our prices."

These setbacks inspired Jon to think outside the box. "I had created the world's first automatic ice dispenser and mated it with the Kold Draft ice machine in 1964, eventually obtaining a patent. I invented the ice dispenser because I had grown tired of shoveling ice.

Jon's first patent — the automatic ice dispenser
paired with a Kold Draft ice machine

"Once I had built the ice dispenser product, I showed it to Kold Draft. I planned to give it to them, but they wanted me to manufacture this product for them. I remember thinking, 'Gee, if they sell 10 per week, and I make $50 on each one, I could make pretty good money.' As it turned out, Kold Draft sold only 10 units every two months or so. What I had created, however, was the first automatic ice dispenser in the country that was sold by a national ice machine manufacturer. I showed Bay City Freezer what I had created, and we sold them the Kold Draft ice machines that included our dispensers. I sold these ice machines and dispensers for years and eventually sold my ice dispenser patent to Kold Draft for $25,000."

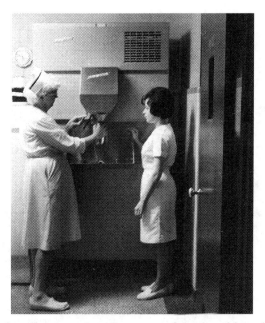

The ice dispenser in use at one of the local hospitals

EDC's competitive advantage was based on low-cost rentals with its built-in service provision feature. While the service feature was profitable, it proved to be a real challenge. Jon says, "I put 75,000 miles a year on my El Camino, driving all over the place servicing our machines. We had no cell phones, so it was not unusual for me to drive to Lansing, service a machine or two, return home, and then get a call that required me to drive back to Lansing for another service call that same day."

One thing that frustrated Jon, which led him to a creative solution, was the fact that service calls would only come in when the bar or restaurant's ice machine was completely out of ice. Employees never seemed to notice that the ice was diminishing and not being replenished, so every service call was urgent. Jon used a clock motor, a ratchet wrench, and a switch that would turn on a light to signify that the ice machine was not producing ice. As the ice dispensed downward, it would force the ratchet device to click down until it ratcheted to its lowest level, and then it would pop back up to the top and repeat the cycle. When the ice stopped hitting the ratchet device, the timing device told the store owner it was time for repair.

From left: Jon's mother, Veronica; brother, Bill Jr.; father, Bill; and Jon at a trade show for EDC circa 1975

Jon began to look for something else to sell because he was running out of customers locally for the products EDC was leasing. He noticed a straight-line conveyor glass washer at a trade show which gave him the idea to start selling glass washers. He then became a dealer. He got a new product to sell by becoming a dealer for Spray Way, a glass washing product built by Moyer Diebold in Canada and distributed by a company named Doll-Flynn, located in Owosso, Michigan. Jon bought from Doll-Flynn and sold his first Spray Way to Arne Walli, owner of Wally's Supper Club in Flint.

Arne Walli was a very special mentor to Jon. He was a restaurateur from Flint, Michigan. Arne opened Walli's Restaurant on Saginaw Street in Flint and eventually Walli's Supper Club directly across the street. He opened his third restaurant on Pierson Road. Jon met Arne when he started renting ice machines to Arne for his restaurants. Despite their 20 year age difference, they ended up becoming lifelong friends until Arne passed away at the age of 93 in 2014. Jon speaks of Arne's mentorship as his gateway to the foodservice industry. "He gave me the freedom to design his fourth restaurant on Center Road near I-69. Arne allowed me to flex my creative muscle while teaching me about the restaurant industry."

Arne Walli

Because the straight-line glass washer was so big and heavy, Jon thought, "Why should people have to walk back and forth to load and unload glasses?" In 1969, he invented the rotary-style glass washer and called it a *Glastender* — a play on the name bartender. This design enabled bartenders to take fewer steps and this, in turn, allowed them to increase their efficiency in executing their duties.

An early photo of Jon's "rotary glasswasher"

Jon sold his first Glastender rotary glass washer to the Ace of Clubs, a bar located on Bay Road in Saginaw (currently the site of Déjà Vu). The second glass washer was developed into a pass-thru cocktail station, installed at Johnson's Bar in Lansing, Michigan.

The pass-thru cocktail station, which introduced a teamwork-oriented approach that doubled bartender output, became an instant success in Michigan. It didn't catch on nationally, as Jon expected, but it opened the door to Jon designing and building a variety of underbar equipment. Glastender started offering its now-famous stainless steel underbar equipment and business began picking up nationally.

One of the very first "rotary glasswashers" ever made

However, according to Jon, "A fundamental problem arose when, after I had done all the legwork in making a sale, the owner of Doll-Flynn would bypass me and sell direct to the customer." Around that same time, Jon shared with the owner his idea for a rotary-style glass washer. He promised to help Jon take his new style glass washer nationally. At that time, Jon did not have manufacturing capabilities. "Instead, the owner took sketches of my design to a manufacturer in Canada. They copied my design and started manufacturing and selling their own rotary glass washers. These copy-cat setbacks taught me a hard lesson."

Phil Compton was a ten-year employee at EDC. He first got to know Jon when he helped him figure a way to put a back seat in Jon's sedan delivery truck. Jon hired Phil in June of 1978 and he worked with EDC until June of 1988, when Jon officially separated Glastender from EDC.

When asked to describe Jon, Phil offered the following: "Jon can be described in one word — visionary! He always keeps his eye on what is important for the customer — never taking his thoughts off the design game. If he can't find what he wants, he makes it! His favorite thing is his design and building work. His hot rod endeavors clearly rely on his design and building talents."

Phil went on to say that Jon is not an easy guy to get to know or understand. "People often see Jon as arrogant. For example, one time when Jon showed up for the Frankenmuth Car Show, they wouldn't give Jon the space he wanted for showing his hot rod, so Jon loaded up the car and took it back home. He really wasn't being arrogant, he simply knew what he wanted and wouldn't settle for less."

According to Phil, "It had been a stressful ten years. The industry was really screwed up. Nothing worked like it was supposed to. 'Go fix it!' was the norm. Ice machines manufactured by other companies would break down due to poorly constructed equipment and a lack of preventative maintenance. This led to continuing service needs. Jon fired me one day for not taking care of a customer who, in my mind, was dead wrong. He re-hired me the next day, but it was clear that Jon insisted on keeping customers happy." Phil remained a business associate and friend, and in 2019, rejoined Jon as an employee of Glastender.

It is important to note that these machines were manufactured by other companies and sold by Jon. The years spent servicing clients played a big part in Jon's motivation to design, build, and sell more automated, maintenance-free equipment. He decided he wanted to be a manufacturer rather than simply a service provider.

Paul Barrera, owner of Jake's Old City Grill restaurant in Saginaw, describes how Jon works with customers: "Jon always focuses on quality, efficiency, and production. We would bounce ideas back and forth about differences between design and reality. He truly listens to people who use his products. With national chains, such as TGI Fridays, Jon would ask 'What do you need and how can we help solve your problem?' Jon excels at listening and then solving problems. He details things with a knowing eye. Jon's capacity for visualization and design is backed by passion!"

Paul does speak from experience when he discusses Jon's character. He has first-hand knowledge of how Jon solves problems with not only efficiency, but also generosity. In 2005, Jon came to Jake's Old City Grill for a late lunch. He noticed that some projects to make the restaurant a viable business were at a standstill because of a lack of funds to complete them. In fact, Paul was close to losing his business. He remembers, "Jon said, 'What will it take to get this Jake's project done?'"

Paul told him that he was about $50,000 short. A few days later, Jon came to the restaurant and asked Paul if he had time to take a short ride. Paul says, "Jon goes into Chase Bank and in a few minutes, returns to the car and hands me an envelope. He says, 'Give me some paperwork on this.' I opened the envelope and it was a $50,000 personal check from Jon. All he wanted was documentation for the loan." Paul had never approached Jon for a loan nor had he asked Jon to be a partner or anything else. Paul says, "I was totally surprised and deeply moved."

Paul adds, "As the Jake's project moved forward, I put in about $40,000 worth of Glastender products, but this was no quid pro quo. I would have used Glastender products anyway!"

Chapter Seven

JON ENLISTS JAY KEGERREIS, A NON-FAMILY EXECUTIVE!

T he hiring of one or more outside executives into a family business can help preserve the value of the family's financial stake in the operation over the long term. To foster this transition, the present CEO must ensure that a new executive can drive progress and hopefully pave the way for family members when they are ready to lead the business.

The late 1970s through the mid-1980s found Jon Hall and his Glastender enterprise facing internal and external challenges. In 1976, Jon had moved Glastender from the original leased factory in downtown Saginaw into a new 12,500-square-foot facility on Agricola Drive in Kochville Township.

The original Glastender facility, taken in the late 1970s

Aerial view of the building on Agricola Drive

Then, in 1977, the economy entered a downward economic spiral. Jon attributes this downturn in the economy to the election of Jimmy Carter as president. To quote Jon, "The most devastating outside pressure came when Jimmy Carter was elected president of the United States." President Carter's term (1977–1981) was extremely bad for our nation's economy — 19% inflation, 22% interest rates, and 70% marginal tax rates. The Carter Administration set a new high for what is called "the misery index."

The misery index is an economic indicator, created by economist Arthur Okun. This index helps determine how the average citizen is doing economically and it is created by adding the seasonally adjusted unemployment rate to the annual inflation rate of a given period. For example, when the inflation rate is running at 15% and unemployment at 8%, the misery index is 23%.

It is assumed that, in combination, a higher rate of unemployment and a worsening rate of inflation creates economic and social costs for a country. The misery index during Carter's administration reached the highest levels of any president in U.S. history. The misery rate was 12.72% when President Carter took office and it was 19.72% when he was defeated by Ronald Reagan, who inherited this very high misery index, yet was able to influence a reduction to a misery index rate of 9.61% over his eight years in office.

A very early ad for Glastender

During these Carter years, according to Phil Compton, "Jon's father was getting old and Jon and Bill had very different opinions regarding how a business should be run. It was obvious that EDC was entering a downward spiral. Like most visionary entrepreneurs, Jon did not particularly enjoy the role of manager. In fact, most entrepreneurial failures are due, not to a defective product or service innovation, but rather due to the lack of strong management practices."

Jon recognized this and rectified the problem by reaching outside the family for help. Jon saw what he needed in a fellow food equipment industry salesman, Jay Kegerreis. Jon met Jay while he was looking for a liquor dispensing system. He liked the liquor system that Jay, the sales manager at Equipment Dispensing, Inc. (EDI), introduced him to. This system included six liquor bottles and a gun. Jon surprised Jay by placing an order for 25 systems. This was a very large order and Jay wondered how Jon would ever sell that many units. Jon had his own plan.

The liquor dispenser held six different types of liquor. When a bottle emptied, it needed to be replaced with a new one. Some customers wanted the ability to have up to three bottles of each type of liquor so the bottles wouldn't need to be replaced so frequently, allowing them to last through entire busy shifts. Although EDI had three-bottle systems, they required a lot of assembly time on the job site. Often times installers set it up any way they could, which did not always look nice. Jon designed an all-in-one cabinet that held all 18 bottles and fit neatly under the bar. In addition, it saved a tremendous amount of installation time. Jon gave his idea to Jay and EDI started making their own to sell.

Jon started buying more products through Jay and joined him in attending an EDI service school. While chatting, they compared notes about how each of them worked 12-plus hours per day.

About this time, ABC, a competitor of EDI, introduced a product that was more sophisticated for larger clientele. ABC introduced a whole new system that made mixed drinks and controlled shot sizes. Their unique selling proposition was "shot size control." Jay left EDI and joined the sales force at ABC.

Jon admired the ABC system but realized that it failed to address the issue of how to efficiently handle the washing and storage of glasses being returned to the bar by the servers. Jon had a ready answer to this challenge.

Specifically, Jon had designed a concept that incorporated glass washers, ice bins, and storage capacity — the cocktail station. Jay was sitting on a $1,000,000 contract for Harrah's Casinos in Las Vegas that did not include a process for handling the dirty glasses. Jay tried to sell Glastender's cocktail station to ABC to resolve this challenge. The cost for an individual sale by ABC would go from $25,000 to $30,000. ABC wouldn't buy it. Jay was so frustrated by what he saw as a lack of vision, he quit ABC.

Jay's leaving ABC opened a window of opportunity for Jon. It was 1978, and he recruited Jay to join Glastender as an investor, vice president, secretary, and treasurer. Jay was a Wake Forest University School of Business graduate and he willingly invested $40,000 for a 10% ownership share of the business. Over time, Jay's share was raised to 25%. When asked why he thought Jay would make a good partner, Jon stated, "He was the only person that wanted to go in the same direction as me." As it turned out, Jay and Jon were the best compliments to each other.

Jon laughs as he describes how he enticed Jay to join Glastender: "Jay had just completed building his new house overlooking Lake Tahoe and was planning to live there because he saw nearby-Las Vegas as offering the best market potential. I enticed Jay to join me at Glastender by saying, 'Look Jay, you work twelve hours a day in Lake Tahoe. Think of all the things you will miss out on while living there and working twelve hours a day. If you move to Saginaw and put in twelve hours per day, you will miss out on less than you will if you live in a resort town like Lake Tahoe.'"

Jay needed to hit the road running because the late seventies had been a stressful time for Glastender and for other businesses nationwide. In the Saginaw area, General Motors' financial problems killed a lot of bar and restaurant businesses. According to Jon, "People simply stopped buying things during Carter's term. Securing a bank loan at 22% interest rate was out of the question. Our profits tanked, and we were forced to reduce our already-small staff."

Phil Compton said, "Jay put the business in the center of the road — creating a kind of cadence for moving Jon's creative ideas from design to profitability. Jon would come up with his next idea and Jay would frequently say things like, 'We need to do this before we do that.'" Jon and Jay had worked through the tough economic times by doing some layoffs and introducing efficiencies wherever they could. It is important to note, however, as Jon points out, "Even when times got the toughest, I never once considered shutting the business down. My response to tough economic times has always been to work harder and smarter."

Jay and Jon at a trade show in the early 1980s

During Jay's early years with Glastender, the product line continued to grow from glass washers to numerous underbar equipment options. Underbar equipment, as the name implies, is the bartender's work station located under the bar top. It contains everything the bartender needs to ice and mix drinks, wash the used glasses, etc.

Challenges, however, had arisen during the 1980s. For example, at one point Jon and Jay had to cancel contracts for all sales reps west of the Mississippi so that Glastender could lower its lead times and keep up with customer demand. By canceling the rep's contracts, Glastender was able to catch its breath and lower its lead time.

It wasn't until August 6, 1982, that Jon was able to draw his first paycheck from Glastender. This marked the beginning of a five-year process to separate himself from EDC. During this time, he exchanged his 50% interest in EDC for his brother Bill's inherited 25% interest in Glastender. This enabled Jon to focus all his efforts on fully exploiting growing demand for his new products.

Jon had decided to trade all his shares in EDC for ownership of Glastender by Jay and himself. Bill assumed responsibility for EDC and the servicing of its existing clients. While Jon recognized the great financial risk associated with his decision, he felt it provided him with the autonomy he needed to design, manufacture, and sell his own products. At the time of the transition, the Equipment Distributing Company was grossing about $750,000 per year while Glastender was grossing only $250,000. However, EDC was entering into a downward spiral. To help EDC survive, Glastender handled the accounting, the front desk, and other day-to-day functions for both companies for the next five years.

Fortunately, by 1983, during President Reagan's term, the economy got back on track and Glastender's business began to pick up. Jon and Jay had started seeing a future that was beginning to look brighter.

Jay at a trade show

There was a flurry of new chain restaurant activity coming on the scene that opened new opportunities for Glastender selling its products. For example, if Jon sold to one individual owner, it was a one-time sale. On the other hand, if he sold to a chain restaurant client, it drove continuous sales for every new store that opened.

In 1984, the first expansion to Glastender's new site was added. This 4,600-square-foot addition to the existing 12,400 square feet brought the total Glastender footprint to 17,000 square feet.

Bank loans, secured via Jay's financial know-how, enabled Glastender to purchase a state-of-the-art Computer Numerically Controlled (CNC) Strippit turret punch machine. This machine punched various shaped holes into sheet metal. This shifted the process from manual hole punching to automated hole punching, thereby making a significant efficiency improvement.

In 1985, Glastender purchased the assets of Cooler Corporation of America, a Florida manufacturing company specializing in keg coolers. This marked Glastender's entry into bar refrigeration.

Jon and Jay outside Cooler Corporation of America

Phil Compton understood what motivated Jon to own and operate Glastender as an entity separate and distinct from EDC. But it didn't make him happy. When the separation happened, Phil resigned from EDC to start his own business, Compton Supply. Phil offered the following comment: "I would still be there if Jon hadn't separated the businesses. I left because I couldn't get along with Jon's brother, Bill, and because we were putting in so many hours that for years, my wife thought I was having an affair!" For entrepreneurs, the business is often the demanding mistress that puts strain on a marriage.

In 1990, Glastender introduced the modular bar die concept that would later become the industry standard. The continued success of the refrigeration line, underbar line, and glass washers prompted the second expansion of the facility in 1990. This expansion of 24,000 square feet to the Glastender facility brought the total square footage to 41,000.

In 1995, the third expansion to the facility added 60,000 square feet for a total of 101,000 square feet. An automatic punching and shearing machine was purchased to nest numerous parts into a single sheet of metal. This eliminated separate shearing and loading of parts. Glastender also started offering a remote draft beer system by purchasing the product line from HABCO Manufacturing out of Toronto, Canada.

Glastender in 2002

According to Jon, despite all these positive developments over the years, "The picture was not all rosy. There were some factors that negatively affected family businesses during this time. For example, business gurus were promoting a focus on quarterly profits as the target. While this focus made shareholders happy, family business owners frequently chose to either sell out to bigger companies or stay with longer-term targets that would sustain their family business over time. Focusing on quarterly profits, in Jay's and my opinion, would be a bad practice for Glastender."

Another challenge, according to Jon, was the hue and cry: "China is coming." Lots of manufacturers simply gave up because they felt they couldn't compete with China's low-cost labor and copy-cat culture. Jon held firmly to the belief that manufacturing is an essential component of economic success and America can compete even if the playing field is not level.

Jay and Jon remained fast friends and a strong business tandem until Jay passed in 1998 at age 49. Jay's passing left a serious managerial void in the Glastender Inc. enterprise.

How would this void be filled?

A DEEPER LOOK INTO JAY'S CHARACTER AND RELATIONSHIPS

According to Phil Compton, "Jay coming on board was a godsend for Jon. He became Jon's closest relationship. Jay brought the business and marketing savvy. He brought badly needed cash as a part of his deal, along with a deep understanding of business economics. Jay's depth of financial knowledge and expertise in business and sales was desperately needed."

Dedicating his professional and analytical qualities to Glastender, Jay produced results and formed business relationships that helped the business grow and succeed in a harsh financial climate. He worked with Linda Marr, who dealt with loans at Manufacturers Bank at the time, and she remembers her first encounter with Jay. "I was immediately impressed with Jay and how he presented things. He walked in with a briefcase and was dressed in a very expensive suit, so I thought, What's in the briefcase? He opens his briefcase and shows me a five-year cash flow projection of what he and Jon, the founder of the business, wanted to do in the future and why they needed a line of credit. Being a loan officer, I had met all kinds of people that didn't come prepared. Jay was totally prepared."

It became a smooth and consistent working relationship, and Linda remembers Glastender began to grow very fast. Jay had insight into the global economy that separated him from many other clients she had. "I continued working with Jay. It seemed like there was a memo on my desk from him on almost a daily basis."

Glastender employees can attest to the character traits that made Jay such a valuable asset and such a pleasure to work with as well. Craig Knuth, a 33-year veteran of the company, remembers what a positive experience it was to work with Jay. "He was very open, honest, upfront with you. Very caring. He was a great guy. I loved working for Jay. My interview with him was unlike any interview that you would ever have with anybody. I mean, it was a three-and-a-half, almost a four hour conversation of just — So what do you like? What do you do? What have you been up to? What kind of jobs have you had? Just an open conversation. And Jay shared a lot about his life, so it just really brought you in and really made you feel like, wow, this guy actually cares. I mean, he remembers my name. He remembers my wife's name, he remembers that I have kids, he remembers it all. He was a very caring person and very genuine."

Zoa May, who began at Glastender as a part-time receptionist in 1982 and retired in the position of purchasing manager after 36 years in 2018, agrees that Jay's skill of recalling the details of a person's life showed what a caring person he was. "Jay had such an amazing memory. He remembered people's names and things about individuals. It was just amazing. He would be at a show and meet somebody he hadn't seen in two, three years and he would know the guy's name, who he worked for, and about his family. I mean, he had just a phenomenal memory."

She recalls what a great partnership Jay and Jon built together as well. "They were such a compliment to each other. Jay understood the finances. But you know, Jon even went to Jay. For example, Jon might say, 'Hey, I need to buy this new machine. It's going to be $30,000.' They always communicated well." She also noticed how their different personalities worked well when dealing with others. "Jon often got frustrated quickly because he's so passionate about everything. And if you don't understand, he doesn't have much patience. Jay was able to deal with people differently. He was able to just handle the fact that people are at different levels."

Rich O'Brien started working for his father's manufacturing company, Gates and O'Brien, as a Glastender rep to work their product line fresh out of college. He remembers, "In April of 1990, my dad went out jogging. He had a heart attack and died. I was probably 24 years old at the time. I was on my own in Kansas City. Jon and Jay told me 'You know, you can do this. We know you're young, but you can do this and we're going to support you.' I kind of flailed around for a few years, trying to figure things out."

During one of Jon's business trips to the area, Rich picked Jon up at the airport and they spent some time together. "Over lunch, he said, 'It's okay if you don't want to do this rep thing. If you're realizing that it's just not what you want, we will support you. Whatever you need, we will support you.'"

Rich decided right then that he wanted to leave the business. He just quit and lived out of his car for a year and a half, spending time out west rock climbing, rabble rousing, and getting into trouble. "One day, Jay called me up. He had Jon on the phone with him. And he said, 'Hey, we're wondering how you're doing. How are things going?' I told them I was doing okay. I don't know [for certain], but Jay was probably sick already by this time. Jon said to me, 'We've got a beer install down in Vale, do you want the job of checking things out for us?' They presented it as if I were doing a favor for them. They told me to just make sure that the cold plates and the beer lines were hooked up, and they told me to have a beer to make sure it tastes good. When I called Jon to assure him everything was in working order, he said, 'Thank you for your services. We will send you a check for five hundred dollars.'

"This example was an indication of who Jon is and how Jon and Jay worked together. They knew that I really wasn't doing anything, but they just needed an excuse to help me out. And that $500 really did help me out at that time. It made me realize that even from a distance and even though I hadn't talked to those guys in 18 months, they were still thinking of me. I think that just kind of shows that Jon has always really cared about the human condition, and even for the offspring of his friends."

Rich realized that it was time to go back into the rep business and back to work for Glastender. "It was a very nice reunion. I am doing well as a Glastender rep now, and Glastender is the gold standard for our industry. That's a testament to Jon, as he has never, ever allowed quality workmanship and performance to slip. Customers know it's top quality, custom built equipment. If they don't want to pay the asking price, that's fine. Get out of the way, because the person behind you has their checkbook out. As reps we are just really very fortunate to continue to work with Glastender. It's wonderful that the family still owns and operates it."

Doug Voeller, of Voeller and Associates, a manufacturer's representative firm in Washington, was hired by Glastender in the 1990s, and was able to observe the working relationship between Jay and Jon up close. "He and Jon were very innovative in different ways. Jon probably needed help on the banking side and with the books and all that stuff. Jon was more interested in designing and building things, fabricating, and just solving mechanical problems. In working with Jay, I found he was always available day or night. Even though we had a time difference of three hours between Seattle and Michigan, I could call Jay at any time and he would pick up.

"One of my favorite stories is about when we started selling cold plates and one of our unique selling propositions was that it never leaked. The first one I sold was to a Chinese restaurant. I get a service call and find that the cold plate is leaking profusely. I can see water just pouring out. It was gushing. I called Jay at 3:30 p.m. my time, 6:30 p.m. his time. I am talking to Jay and all of the sudden I hear Jon's voice. His words were, 'I want it back. I want to find out exactly where it failed, and we will assure you it will never happen again.' Since then I have never found one leak over the past 20-30 years, and that's the way Glastender continues to do things. We found out, as we got into their product line, that Glastender simply built better products than its competitors. Glastender was a more innovative, higher-quality manufacturer. We simply had better product. And over the time, we just got very comfortable selling a better product, and we would go find the customers that appreciate quality."

Jay's death was taken as a deeply-felt loss by the Hall family. He had been woven into the fabric of the company as a partner to Jon, a mentor to the Hall children, and the engine that made the management team function. He was a command and control leader who complemented and supported Jon's design and manufacturing creativity. Zoa May cried while remembering, "We were all so heartbroken that we cried when we discovered that he had brain cancer because it took away all of that. When Jay passed, we really weren't sure how we would survive. Jay just was involved in so many things. We weren't really sure what was going to happen.

"I feel bad for the people that hired in after Jay passed away, because they didn't get to know what a great man he was. I love the fact that the Halls not only respected him and worked with him, but loved him, and they never let people forget about Jay. He's never going to be forgotten."

Chapter Eight

THE KIDS TAKE OVER!

"Shirtsleeves to shirtsleeves in three generations" is the adage that characterizes many family-owned and -operated businesses. Only 30% of family-owned businesses are still viable into the second generation. Since the family business is managed primarily for the inter-generational transfer of asset ownership and/or control, this is not a promising statistic.

With Jay's passing, the viable continuation of Glastender into the second generation would fall into the hands of Jon's son, Todd; daughter, Kim; and son-in-law Mark Norris. Taking the standards and qualities they learned from their father, they carried on the foundations of generosity in business, exceptional customer experience, and building relationships. This trio became true game changers.

Kim, Todd, and Jon in 2007
Photo courtesy of The Rehmann Group

* * *

A distinguishing feature between a family business and a non-family business is *nepotism*. Nepotism was originally defined as "the hiring of relatives of the owner of a business." Today, the definition is "the existence of employees within an organization that are related to each other by blood or marriage."

Issues raised by nepotism are favoritism, discipline, fraud, confidentiality, and personal issues. Yet, there are also positives related to the issue of nepotism, e.g. lower recruiting costs, lower training costs, lower employee turnover, higher level of loyalty, higher level of morality, and higher trust levels.

* * *

The negative factors associated with nepotism are clearly not present with respect to the second generation of Glastender's management team. In fact, the Hall family has always created an environment to produce a family-like atmosphere among the employees. "Almost every CEO says,

'We have a family culture.' Almost none of them really do," comments Pete Light, a 40-year veteran of Glastender and the most tenured employee (next to Jon). "When something goes wrong, and it's going to cost them money, you're gone!" But at Glastender, Pete credits the formation and continuation of the culture to the Hall family. "It's such a long history of culture. But I think it's the entire family, to be honest; they manage it top down. I mean, Jon, obviously, drives a lot of that culture and raised his kids to treat people well and be concerned about other people, and not necessarily themselves or just their pocketbook. And so, as Todd and Kim have taken over the company, they've really created a place to be one that wants people to feel like family."

Factors such as continuity of purpose, committed and engaged people, and effective and efficient operational and sales processes have also enabled the success of the transition to this second-generation management team.

What this team has done is slowly and methodically unfolded processes and systems that have shifted the paradigm of management at Glastender from a highly-centralized command and control structure to an employee engagement model. This shift didn't come about without some serious pain. The stakes were high, but if successful, Glastender would join a unique group of multi-generational family-owned and -operated businesses. For example:

- John Brooke and Sons, a United Kingdom-based firm established in 1541, is now headed by Mark Brooke, a 15th-generation family member.
- Craig Zildjian and his sister, Debbie Zildjian, jointly head the 14th-generation Zildjian Cymbal Company, the well-known cymbal smiths, located in Massachusetts.
- In Italy, third-generation Agnellis control Fiat and now Chrysler. In France, the Peugeot heirs control the company.
- In Germany, the second-generation Quandt family members own 46% of the BMW shares.
- In Japan, CEO Akio Toyoda, at 59 years of age, is the youngest family member on the board of the Toyota Corporation.

- In the United States, fourth-generation Ford executive chairman, William Clay Ford, serves alongside non-family CEO Jim Hackett.

In all the above examples (and there a many more), there were interested and able next-generation family members. This was also the case with Glastender.

A Profile of Successful Successors was presented at the HSM Global Family Business Forum in Mexico City in 2010 by Davis J. Successor Development. Let's look at these criteria with respect to the Hall family business:

CRITERION 1: THEY KNOW THE BUSINESS WELL AND LIKE OR LOVE THE NATURE OF THE BUSINESS.

Fortunately, key second-generation members of the Hall family had worked part time with Glastender. Kim and Todd were willing to gain on-the-job know-how. Mark Norris (Kim's spouse) joined Glastender in 1993, after working at Fullerton Tool, his previous place of employment. Todd, Kim, and Mark now oversee all aspects of the business and, together, they demonstrate a sincere commitment to controlled growth and profitability.

CRITERION 2: THEY KNOW THEMSELVES AND THEIR STRENGTHS AND WEAKNESSES, HAVING THE NECESSARY EXPERIENCE AND EDUCATION.

The leadership team of Todd, Kim, and Mark are all keenly aware of their own and of each other's strengths and weaknesses. They have demonstrated a willingness to make commitments together and to declare a breakdown when it appears that a commitment is not being fulfilled.

CRITERION 3: THEY WANT TO LEAD AND SERVE.

The Hall family leadership team enjoys their roles as leaders. No one is along for the ride. Role delineation is clear, yet they share an understanding of each other's responsibilities and work to ensure cross-unit coordination.

CRITERION 4: THEY ARE GUIDED RESPONSIBLY BY THE PREVIOUS GENERATION, BY ADVISERS, AND BY A BOARD OF OUTSIDE ADVISORS.

Jon Hall founded Glastender and continues to drive product design and quality. The entire Glastender workforce recognizes and appreciates this. In 2016, the Hall family added three outside advisors to their governance structure. The governance structure of Glastender consists of the Advisory Board, which is made up of Jon, Todd, Kim, Richard Hall, and three outside Advisory Board members: Joe Schmieder, Family Business Consulting Group; Paul Dege, Oliver Supply Company (RET); and Tim Liang, Alpha Max Consulting.

CRITERION 5: THEY HAVE GOOD RELATIONSHIPS AND THE ABILITY TO ACCOMMODATE OTHERS, ESPECIALLY IF PART OF A SUCCESSOR TEAM (SIBLINGS, IN-LAW, COUSINS).

This quality has been exemplified by the assimilation of Mark Norris into the fabric of the leadership team in 1993 prior to Kim, who started in 1996. Todd, just out of college, had joined the firm in 1991. Kim and Todd both worked for the company as teenagers. Jon's willingness to let his children shape their own roles was remarkable. In turn, they make accommodations and encourage flexibility with their employees as well. "It's rare to find some place that you can be brought in, made to feel like family, given the keys to the kingdom, do your thing," said Craig Knuth. "Nobody questions what you're doing, how you're doing it, why you're doing it. I mean, they just give you a lot of time. I needed autonomy to really run loose with things and make it my own. So that's what I like too, that they really value what you bring to the table. It's not a micromanage situation by any stretch of imagination."

CRITERION 6: THEY CAN COUNT ON COMPETENT NON-FAMILY MANAGERS IN THE TOP MANAGEMENT TEAM TO COMPLEMENT THEIR OWN SKILL.

Just as Jay Kegerreis brought sales and financial acumen from the outside, Mark brought a performance toughness that was and is needed in overseeing a manufacturing operation. Mark is given free rein to make the manufacturing operation hum like one of Jon's hot rods.

CRITERION 7: THEY HAVE CONTROLLING OWNERSHIP OR CAN LEAD THROUGH ALLIES AS IF THEY DO.

The Glastender business is fully controlled by the Hall family bloodline.

CRITERION 8: THEY HAVE EARNED THE RESPECT OF NON-FAMILY EMPLOYEES, SUPPLIERS, CUSTOMERS, AND OTHER FAMILY MEMBERS.

The second-generation Glastender enterprise demonstrates its commitment to treating all employees as part of a large family. The leadership team works extremely hard to generate employee performance buy-in. The team puts its money where its mouth is through its bonus program based on company profits.

Human Resource Manager Michelle Thurlow says, "I have been working at Glastender for 21 years. Glastender is a great family business. It treats its non-family employees at all levels as extended family. Everyone here feels valued. The leadership wants us to keep growing. There are lots of internal promotions based on employee performance and their aspirations. I look at Glastender as a 'we organization.' I always refer to Glastender as 'we.' I can't imagine working any other place. To leave here, they would have to kick me out!"

Ann Lopez is serving as senior human resource professional. "I have been working at Glastender since 2000 — 20 years. I feel fortunate to be a part of the Glastender family. And it is a family. As an example, when Michelle [Thurlow] was pregnant, Glastender hired my mother on 'temporary assignment.' She worked here for seven years. When mom died, Kim drove me to the hospital, and the entire Hall family attended her funeral. I will never forget that. We have a true family culture here and I am delighted to be a part of it."

Employee turnover rates have remained impressive, running between 4-10% over the past five years in an industry known to have turnover of 20% or more.

CRITERION 9: THEIR SKILLS AND ABILITIES FIT THE STRATEGIC NEEDS OF THE BUSINESS.

Jon has a keen eye for what will make the jobs of customers easier and he creatively designs products to meet these needs. His unique designs have become industry-leading models for competitors to follow. Todd has deep product and sales knowledge. Kim focuses on the human side of the enterprise. Mark runs the manufacturing operation. Together, with their respective teams, they have designed and implemented strategies that encompass the best knowledge and experience of their combined talents.

CRITERION 10: THEY RESPECT THE PAST AND FOCUS THEIR ENERGIES ON THE FUTURE OF THE BUSINESS AND THE FAMILY.

Glastender is in it to win it. The goal is to keep the business productive and profitable, so they can provide future generations of family and employees with a place to earn a living and build a good life.

Phil Compton believes the structure of the bonus program and the systems put in place by the family have contributed to the success of the business. "The leadership team has done a good job here of fixing that high stress environment that existed when I worked at EDC all those years ago. They're patient about growing the business. They've got the structure down, so that the company can make money and the employees can make a good living." Their definition of success also includes unsurpassed service to their customers, strong partnerships with vendors, and giving back to their community.

While most employees understand what it took to get Glastender where it is today, Jon continually reminds his people that he is not focused on the rear-view mirror. He is, and he wants everybody else to be, focused on the future. He sees that future as very, very bright.

Focusing on a bright future was a habit that Jon developed over time, and with help. Jon's brother-in-law, Louie Furlo, became a mentor. Louie also possessed great business acumen. He acquired and built Morley Companies into an extremely successful family-owned and -operated enterprise that serves an international client base. According to Jon, "Louie was always positive, constantly acquiring new knowledge, and never shied away from trying new things. He taught me that my thoughts and attitude would shape my future."

Jon recalls, "Louie gave me the audio book *The Strangest Secret*, by Earl Nightingale, wherein he explained 'You become what you think about all day long.' He further explained that the subconscious mind is a rich fertile field not tethered to facts, fiction, right or wrong, so whatever you plant there will grow. But you had to think about it. Nightingale suggested writing ten things on 3x5 cards and looking at them every day."

These writings strongly influenced Jon's thinking as he moved forward. The key thought was, "We are what we think about all day." Jon applied the thought processes of high-performance people espoused by Nightingale and others, which became the foundation of Jon's unique approach to unleashing his potential in business and in life. Jon says, "We can grow, but to do so we must be at it every day."

Passing the torch on to his children demonstrates Jon's belief in the future success of the business because he knows it is passing into safe hands. The triumvirate management team of Todd, Kim, and Mark has led the charge to fully professionalize the Glastender business. Together they oversee all business operations. Jon has willingly relinquished the reigns of leadership, thereby enabling him to focus on creative product design, along with his core of engineers.

Chapter Nine

THE SECOND-GENERATION HALL FAMILY MOSAIC

G lastender could be viewed as a third-generation business if looked at as an extension of Equipment Distributing Company (EDC). Jon, however, prefers to see Glastender as a second-generation business because of the shift from a distributing company to a manufacturing business. For purposes here, Glastender can be thought of as a second-generation family-owned and -operated business.

Jon remains the lead design person, supported by a cast of engineers. He has relinquished day-to-day management to the very capable hands of Todd, Kim, and Mark. Richard and Kristina are shaping careers within Glastender, while Jon Jr. has created his own business.

TODD HALL

Todd Hall is a rock and roll singer and romantic songwriter at heart. Just as Jon loves his hot rods, Todd is passionate about his music. As lead singer of the band Riot V, he manifests the attributes of creativity, enthusiasm, high self-esteem, networking, physical stamina, presentation skills, and talent. He exudes all these qualities as he performs his responsibilities as president of Glastender.

Hicks Studio

Todd is as comfortable representing Glastender products and services to prospects at food industry manufacturing trade shows as he is when he performs with his band. With his youthful appearance, long hair, and casual dress, he looks more like a rock star than he does the president of a multimillion-dollar manufacturing company. He frequently refers to his musical engagements in his presentations to customers and employees. From his perspective, he is the lead singer of Glastender, surrounded and supported by a harmonious and talented cast of managers and employees.

Academically, Todd has excelled. He earned the title of class valedictorian of his Arthur Hill High School graduating class of 1987. He also graduated with honors from the University of Michigan's School of Business in 1991.

Todd began early as he developed his song writing, singing, and performance skills. He started out playing local rock and roll venues in and around Saginaw with brother Jon Jr. He now performs, mostly overseas, with Riot V, originally formed in 1975, which Todd joined in 2013. On the more romantic side, he recently created and released an album consisting of songs inspired by his years-long pen pal relationship with his future wife, Lumpeny (Nönö), who lived in India. He donated the proceeds of the sales to Rescue Ministries of Mid-Michigan.

According to his mom Brenda, "Todd is a very spiritual person and a great singer. He can rock with the best of them and then write and sing Christian songs. I think he was born with an old soul. He is spiritual, but not fanatical."

Like his siblings Jon Jr., Kim, Richard, and Kristina, Todd worked part time at Glastender while in high school and college. He started full time in sales in 1991, following a path from sales associate to sales manager to vice president. In 2008, he assumed the role of president. This rise in ranks within the company comes as no surprise to those that know Todd well and have witnessed his character and leadership throughout his life. "The minute I saw Todd, and I saw him when he was 14 years old, I knew he was going to become the president," stated Zoa May. "I knew it from what Jon said. And I knew it from the way Todd was just interacting here, picking up stuff. He is detailed, very smart about everything he does."

Todd has become a very adept spokesperson with deep product knowledge, a full understanding of what it takes to drive sales, and a strong business understanding that emanates from his Business and Management Degree. He does a masterful job of explaining the features and benefits of Glastender products and services at events such as the North American Association of Food Equipment Manufacturers (NAFEM) trade show.

Among the employees of Glastender, Todd has a reputation of caring for the relationship with each person he works with. Zach Fowler says, "I'm up in sales, and I've been here for about six years. I think Todd's the biggest cheerleader out of everybody. He takes everything so personally. He wants everybody to be happy, which is great. You see his face. You don't know the president of any company going around and personally making sure that everybody's on the same page [like Todd does]. His style is very much *management by walking around*. And if you ever have a problem, then it's only a problem if you don't say anything."

It is apparent to those that work with Glastender that the same standards of highest quality customer experience and building

REBEL WITHOUT APPLAUSE • 77

relationships with employees and clients alike that Jon valued have been carried on in Todd. Frank Pfisterer of Tine Design, a food service design and consulting business, commented on his working relationship with Glastender, saying "Jon's a brilliant guy, you know, there's no question. He's a creator and innovator and a classic: he's a great businessman. He's enjoyable, it's nice to be around him, and he cares about what he's doing. I have to say that the same passion really kind of rolled over into Todd; then Todd has his own unique way of approaching it, too. And that's what makes them amazing to deal with, not only as a company, but as a family. And I don't really distinguish the two. For me, I just feel like I'm dealing with a family. And that's what's nice about it."

KIMBERLY (HALL) NORRIS

Kim (Hall) Norris earned her bachelor's degree in 1989 and her master's degree in 1998 from Saginaw Valley State University School of Nursing.

Leaving her nursing career to join Glastender in October of 1996 was intended to be a temporary move to assist her father as Jay battled brain cancer. The frame of reference she brought to the job was to provide a calm hand and a cool head in the emergency faced by her father. Her most important task was to address the human resource and safety functions. She immediately embarked on a quest to create a caring and just culture — one that does not hold workers accountable for system failures. At the same time, it was necessary to ensure that reckless behavior would not be tolerated. Embedded in her thinking was the belief that the most important function of her job was to address the human aspect of the business.

Kristina said, "I'm really impressed with Kim. I think she's really orchestrating the human side of the enterprise, so to speak. And that's what HR should do. Sometimes she's the lubricant that reduces friction and makes things work smoother. But, at other times, she's the glue that holds things together."

Kim became the heart of Glastender.

Hicks Studio

Kim is both able and willing to act on her sensibilities. Her ready smile and lively sense of humor enable her to shift gears in a nanosecond, moving from an exploratory discussion to possibilities and then to action.

What started out as a temporary assignment changed when Kim was named vice president of administration in 2008, overseeing the functions of the human resources department, accounting, information technology, and safety. She would also play a shared leadership role with Jon, Todd, and Mark in shaping the governance and management structures of Glastender.

Leadership styles differed markedly between Kim and Jay Kegerreis. He was a perfectionist who had difficulty delegating work and commensurate decision-making authority. Simply stated, like the wheel on a bicycle, all spokes led to Jay as the hub. Kim saw a need to define management roles and responsibilities in ways that vested authority and accountability that matched job titles.

After meeting with employees, she identified an urgent need to address the lack of systems and processes throughout the organization. Implementing a more professional business structure to match the needs of a growing business was not immediately met with enthusiasm by the workforce. It didn't take long for Kim to realize that people don't resist change as much as they resist being changed. As someone once said, "The only one who really wants to be changed is a wet baby!"

The aroma of accountability drifted across the organization. Kim hired a consulting group to assist in analyzing the current workplace context and in designing an efficacious management structure. Her efforts in this domain led her dad to affectionately saddle her with the moniker "Colonel Clink" — seeing the world through black and white lenses with little or no gray with respect to most issues.

The facts do not bear out the "Colonel Clink" label. While Kim remained undeterred to shift the organization from what she saw as chaos to order, she held firmly to the belief that employees benefit personally when systems and structures are in place. With continuous improvement based on best practice research and on-site observation, she readily calls out deficient performance but always offers help to bring a person's performance up to industry and Glastender expectations.

Culture trumps strategy. An engaged workforce is the desired outcome of employee training and development initiatives. Glastender is now a model of employee engagement.

MARK NORRIS

Mark Norris joined the company in May of 1993, shortly after Todd but before Kim came on board. He was recruited by Jon, Jay, and Todd. For several years, Mark had worked for Morgan and Dick Curry, the owners of Saginaw-based Fullerton Tool.

According to Mark, "I loved my job with Fullerton Tool. I had started dating Kim, and for the first three years of our relationship, I had never even visited Glastender. One day, I needed some tables for an event. Jon offered to provide the tables. Jon showed me around and began probing me about my career goals. His motive, as it turned out, was to hire me. I was married to Kim by that time and I decided to sit down with Jon and Jay to hear what they had to offer. I also talked with Todd."

Mark went on to say, "I was extremely reluctant to leave Fullerton Tool. Morgan and Dick Curry had a great family business and treated me very well. I was also concerned about possible nepotism complications of joining a family business now that I was a part of the family.

"What drew me to Glastender was my assessment that it was a business with greater opportunity for professional growth for myself. The bar equipment manufacturing industry, in my mind, offered more career opportunities than the tooling industry because, at the time, there were not as many bar equipment manufacturers as there were cutting tool manufacturers. In addition, I had gained useful knowledge about sheet metal fabrication while working summers during college at Saginaw Control and Engineering. I felt that basic knowledge provided a good foundation for further developing my skills and knowledge necessary to make a serious contribution to the success of Glastender.

"I started out in charge of inventory control. At first, I felt like someone had shipped me to Mars. The plant was chaotic. The lack of accountability allowed for bad behavior of some employees. While I had some experience at driving out waste and inefficiencies, I really invested time and energy in learning all I could about lean manufacturing practices. I learned from various sources, such as the first consultants we brought in, and from reading several books, most notably *The Goal* by Eliyahu M. Goldratt. Working with Kim and Todd, we figured out what needed to be done and did it."

From my observation, Mark brought a frame of reference akin to that of many NFL head football coaches I have worked with. He clearly believes in pre-game preparation and post-game analysis as essential ingredients in the highly competitive and unforgiving game of manufacturing. In Mark's own words, "I believe in metrics — numbers that tell us useful things about efficiencies and productivity. I can know in fifteen minutes how well we did yesterday. I can see days of inventory. I can see how many dollars in incoming sales, and all the key performance indicators (KPI) for manufacturing operations."

Mark also believes, as all good NFL coaches do, that perfect practice makes perfect. He believes that managing the practice routine gives him a chance to see that needed adjustments will be done correctly

— and quickly. Mark also knows what talent he needs to make the manufacturing process both efficient and effective. He is no shrinking violet in calling out poor performance. He is direct and demanding.

Hicks Studio

Mark's efforts led to his being given expanded responsibilities and commensurate authority over time. He became plant manager in 1998, followed by a promotion to vice president of operations in 2008.

An NFL coach needs to manage his assistant coaches as well as his players. As vice president of operations, his key responsibilities include strategic oversight of production, purchasing, engineering, and inside sales. His ability to visualize his end goal, then develop and execute a strategic action plan, is remarkable. His impact on the profitability of the company is not easily quantifiable but significant. He is a very important player in the Hall family business enterprise.

RICHARD HALL

Richard Hall (Rick) is the computer whiz of the Hall clan. His interest in playing video games led him to ask his parents to buy him a computer at age thirteen so he could play video games at home. In spite of the cost and a general lack of knowledge about computers, his mom and dad bought Rick his first computer, an Atari 800. A problem arose when Rick couldn't afford to buy the games he wanted. Fortunately, the computer contained a BASIC programming language cartridge that allowed him to create his own games while experimenting with computers. Learning to make the computer do things opened a whole new world of possibilities beyond just playing games.

Jay Kegerreis brought 16-year-old Rick into Glastender in 1985 to show him how to set up a new accounting system. Jay had little or no knowledge with respect to software implementation or computer programming. Later, when Rick returned home for summers while earning his undergraduate degree at the University of Michigan, he continued to offer IT guidance to Jay.

Once Rick completed his undergraduate degree in computer engineering in 1990, he enrolled at the University of Colorado's School of Engineering to get his master's degree. He completed his degree in 1993, at which time he took a job with Johns Hopkins University's Applied Physics Lab in Laurel, Maryland. He didn't find the work interesting or challenging, so he decided to return to the University of Colorado and pursue his Ph.D. in Computer Science.

During the summers, Rick would return to work at Glastender — this time, on the manufacturing side of the business. His efforts were directed toward developing a Materials Resource Planning (MRP) system to manage the ordering and picking of parts to be used for completing jobs and for enabling better inventory control. One problem he discovered was that people were making a lot of counting mistakes. Implementing a commercial MRP system was a huge and expensive undertaking. There was fear in undertaking such a system without having a better understanding of what was needed and how it might work at Glastender. Because of this, Rick developed a makeshift MRP system that was useful until the company had a better understanding of what was needed in a commercial MRP system.

Rick successfully completed his Ph.D. in Computer Science in 1999 and promptly moved to Europe. During this period (2000 – 2008), Rick served as an assistant professor at Free University in Berlin, Germany, and he taught and did research at Joseph Fourier in Grenoble, France. On re-entering the United States, Rick served a one-year stint at Tufts University in Medford, Massachusetts, as a visiting professor.

While Rick was working in France, he enrolled in a French class at a nearby university where he met Ya-ching Liang, a native of Taiwan, who was enrolled in the same class. They eventually married and returned to Saginaw in 2008 to start a family. Rick is now adding his technology skills to the work flow at Glastender.

Because of his varied experiences in his professional background, Kim explains how important Rick's contribution is to the enterprise in ways even beyond his technology skills, saying "He is a great wordsmith, and anytime we're doing something, we try to run it by Rick and get his point of view on it, because he brings a lot of professionalism into how to communicate and a lot of outsider perspective. He's got a really good analytical mind. He's added so much value to the management team."

KRISTINA (HALL) KELCHERMAN

Kristina (Hall) Kelcherman graduated from high school in 2001, enrolled at Delta College, then transferred later to The Art Institute of Orange County, California. After receiving her degree, she lived in Costa Mesa where she was working for a shoe retailer, eventually becoming the distribution manager. In 2013, she returned to Saginaw and joined Glastender's workforce on a part-time basis.

Kristina is using her degree in graphic art and her artistic talents serving first as the company's videographer and most recently becoming a full-time digital media specialist.

JON HALL JR.

Jon Hall Jr., the first child of Jon and Brenda Hall, was born in 1965. Those who know him well argue that he is the most like his father. Unlike his siblings, he prefers to work independently of the Glastender business. He has started his own business, called Phat Cat Guitars, wherein he focuses his creative efforts on selling and servicing guitars and other music industry products.

He is a bit introverted, but once he opens up, he reveals an interesting persona and, like his father, limits most discussions to those things he is passionate about, which, in his case, is music and all things associated with it. He also loves cars and motorcycles. I found him to be both knowledgeable and conversational when we talked about music, guitars, famous bands, cars, and motorcycles. Zoa May explained, "Jon Jr. is a lot like his dad. And he finally found what he really needed to find with his guitar shop."

If the conversation turns too personal, he tends to withdraw. One exception was a discussion about his daughter. He is proud of Amaya and tries to be a very good dad — a not-too-easy task for any parent when it comes to co-parenting a teenage daughter.

Jon Jr. did not get his nickname "Junior" from his family. That moniker was hung on him by the employees of Glastender while he was working part time as a teenager. Why? Simply because he was the son of founder and CEO Jon Hall.

* * *

Being labeled with sometimes-unwanted monikers in family businesses is not uncommon. I remember when I was doing executive coaching for a third-generation beer and wine distributing company in the state of Washington, the employees labeled the succeeding CEOs, all named Sid, as "El Sid," "Mid-Sid," and "Kid-Sid."

Chapter Ten

CULTURE EATS STRATEGY!

In an article of the January/February 2018 issue of *Harvard Business Review* entitled "The Culture Factor," there is the quote, "As someone once said, culture eats strategy for breakfast." We now hear that quote attributed to people like Tom Brady, quarterback of the New England Patriots, and a host of others. The reason it is so often quoted is that it rings true. Culture includes things like shared beliefs, expectations, attitudes, and values — the stuff that's hard to codify and certainly hard to evaluate and, therefore, hard to manage. Many experts, such as Peter Senge, author of *The Fifth Discipline*, and John P. Kotter, author of *Leading Change*, have added to the understanding with complex and nuanced constructs.

This invisible nature of culture causes many managers to treat culture as a soft topic, but it's the stuff that determines how we get things done. Todd defers to Kim on the issue of culture when he says, "Kim came from a bigger company that was more professionally developed than Glastender. While I had graduated with a business degree from the University of Michigan, all I knew about running the business was what I had been shown by Dad or Jay. I am not trying to denigrate what they had accomplished, but nothing was formalized, and the culture had formed by drift rather than by design. Glastender needed to evolve into a more professional organization with clear roles and responsibilities, systems and structure, and employee engagement. When I started with Glastender, we only had 28 employees, so as we grew, a more formal approach was needed."

One of the things Kim did when she joined Glastender was to get the managers to sit together as a team. According to Kim, "While there were manager titles, they were never delegated a lot of authority. I wanted to see managers who had authority and responsibility that matched their job title. The first thing I did was write job descriptions. I wrote one for Mark, who was already functioning as plant manager — but without a job description. I made his title official."

Once Kim got the job titles confirmed and the manager meetings underway, she brought groups of 20 employees together (there were 100 employees in all) and asked them to each respond to three questions, namely:

- What do you love about Glastender?
- What do you hate about Glastender?
- What would you wish for at Glastender?

After aggregating and studying the results, Kim went to Jon and Jay and announced, "There is a lot of chaos going on around here. We need more than just HR policies and procedures." Even then, employees expressed their love for the organization and the family-like culture, but at the same time they felt frustration over the lack of organization in plant operations.

Shortly thereafter, Kim heard about a speaker coming to Saginaw Valley State University who would be talking about lean manufacturing. It was a short half-day program that she asked her dad to attend. Kim adds, "Any longer than that, Dad would have refused to go, but he did, and he liked what he heard. He especially bought into the need for employee engagement and the point that managers always throw resources at problems instead of looking at the process. When something goes wrong, there is a tendency to point fingers at people, when it is really a process or systems problem." Looking at these two issues was a big take-away for Jon.

Kim points out, "We engaged the consulting firm that conducted the half-day program and proceeded to spend a lot of time and money having employees sit in classrooms learning about the importance of establishing current best processes. We engaged the employees in some simulation games that focused on the importance of excellent work flow and on removing bottlenecks. This lean-manufacturing training and employee involvement was the bedrock of the strategic thinking that would come to permeate our company. However, it took fifteen years before lean manufacturing was truly up and running at Glastender."

One reason many companies frequently avoid offering training is because it requires time off the job. When asked about this, Todd quickly offered, "Time off the job for employee training is essential. You can't expect employees to go along with a change unless they understand what the change is about and are engaged in the process."

One factor in the slow assimilation of lean manufacturing was the fact that Todd wasn't all-in on what was going on at the time. Todd explains, "I was too busy managing the sales process. This was a problem because if you are the leader and you are not living and breathing what is being implemented, it will never work. You can't turn everything over to consultants and expect them to pull it off without your engagement. We had told the consultants early on that what they were teaching us wasn't impossible, but very difficult for us given our skill sets, talents, and processes at the time. The main reason it took us many years to turn things around was that we had a whole host of things that needed to be in place first."

Another challenge, Kim adds, was "getting Dad to realize he had to change too. While analyzing our production processes, we discovered that Dad negatively impacted on-time delivery. When we explained to Dad that he could no longer interrupt press brake operators any time he felt like it to have them bend up a prototype part he was working on for R&D, he wasn't very happy. Needless to say, there were times I started to feel we would never be able to climb this mountain and realize success."

Although a great deal of time was spent putting employees through training to help them understand what the company was trying to accomplish, it was very challenging for them. For the first time ever, employees were being asked for a lot of input. They were asked to collect data during their day for the purpose of identifying areas where better processes could be established.

Resistance to change mounted. This, coupled with Todd not being fully invested, led to a great deal of frustration. Unfortunately, the combination of a lack of strong leadership and employee resistance led the leadership team to abandon the program from the consultants. They were not, however, abandoning what they learned from them — the need for a clear strategic plan, employee engagement, and focused attention on eliminating waste through process improvements. The consultants also helped Todd to see that he needed to pull himself away from the day-to-day work so he could work *on* the business, not just *in* the business. In an effort to move in that direction, Todd was named vice president in 1999 and additional sales staff were added so he could transition fully into a leadership role.

Triggered by all the chaos at the end of 1999, the Teamsters attempted to unionize the workforce. Kim immediately called in a consulting group specializing in helping businesses work through a union campaign. The first thing the consultants did was walk around surveying each employee. They gave the leadership team a summary report that did not reveal the names of the responding employees, but did rank the concerns from the most frequently stated complaints to the least.

Specifically, 55% of the employees said that the changes made under the guidance of the consultants were "leading to the downfall of the company." While character and trust were never questioned, employees simply didn't like what they were going through.

Glastender defeated the unionization effort. The final vote was 61 to 30. However, there was a side effect that created additional challenges. The following year, Glastender saw a 50% employee turnover followed by a 30% turnover rate the year after that. While the unionization vote triggered some of this turnover, there were other factors. One such factor was that automotive companies were hiring and still had the reputation of $30-per-hour pay rates.

Today, when Todd and Kim look back at the old employee survey data, they enjoy a laugh at such comments as, "We want raises, not a bonus program." Kim recently showed the top complaints to employees and asked, "Does that sound like Glastender today?" The answer was a resounding, "No!"

One good thing the consultants had done was suggest to Todd he needed to move into Jay's old office as a symbolic shift. Regarding this message, Kim says, "We needed a leader, and by 2000, Todd was ready. He was on-board with needed changes and had more available time to address them."

Shortly after, Todd read the book *Harley-Davidson: The Complete History* by Darwin Holmstrom that detailed the motorcycle company's survival through challenging times. With ideas gleaned from the book, Todd wanted to create a new strategy. A crucial factor in moving out of all the chaos was getting Beth McMall from Rehmann Consulting Group involved. She was asked to conduct a strength, weaknesses, opportunities, and threats (SWOT) analysis that involved all of management. As a part of this analysis, all participants were asked to answer the following four questions:

1. Why does Glastender exist?
2. What values do we hold as an organization?
3. Where do we want the company to be in five to ten years?
4. What are the things we need to do to get there?

Later, breakout sessions were conducted with all employees, asking the same questions. The results were amazing. Glastender's core values showed up throughout. Having a family culture was at the top, yet they did not consider it a core value at the time.

The core values that emerged were:

1. Quality with pride
2. Integrity without compromise
3. Valuing relationships
4. Creatively driving continuous improvement

From these core values, Glastender's central purpose was formed:

❝ Manufacturing creative solutions by doing it first or doing it better."

With the guiding values and strategic focus identified, the next thing to tackle was how to make it happen. Glastender's management team implemented two powerful initiatives that contributed to professionalizing the company:

1. Process Based Leadership
2. Open Book Management

These initiatives will be discussed in the following two chapters.

Chapter Eleven

PROCESS BASED LEADERSHIP

M ark read the book *Buried Alive! Digging Out of a Management Dumpster* by Anna VerSteeg, Debra Boggan, John Pyecha, Lina Segall, and Shane Yount (April 2004). He wanted to implement what he had read with his production supervisors. When Kim reviewed what Mark wanted to do with his team, she suggested that they do it with the whole company. To gain a more comprehensive understanding of Process Based Leadership (PBL), Kim and Todd flew to a conference in Cincinnati, Ohio. Process Based Leadership was presented by Shane Yount, one of the authors of the book. His company is called Competitive Solutions, Inc.

In a nutshell, PBL is a management system that provides clear direction, connects everyone to the same goals, and is consistent throughout all levels of management. Ultimately, it provides accountability and a sense of urgency throughout the organization.

Todd, Kim, and Mark made a conscious decision at the start to be fully committed to the implementation of PBL. They knew employees would not accept the change if management wasn't walking the walk themselves. It was implemented within the management ranks over an eighteen-month period to ensure that leadership was fully engaged before they introduced PBL to the employees.

What does Glastender mean by Process Based Leadership? According to Todd:

- We form teams based on their role within the company.
- We have regular meetings that revolve around a business scorecard rooted in our strategic plan.
- We develop strategic actions based on our review of the scorecard.
- We follow up on previous actions to make sure they were completed.
- Our goal is to reach our targets through discipline and focus.
- For us to be successful, we must have the engagement and involvement of all employees.
- We begin with the management team and follow a top-down implementation format. For example, the process began with the managers and did not go down to the supervisor level until there was confidence that the process was fully adopted by the executive leadership team.
- The primary role of the management team is to set the strategic direction for the company and to ensure that all employees are part of a team and adhere to the process.
- The various aspects of Process Based Leadership have certain governing rules, which are called non-negotiables, because everyone must follow these rules.
- The business scorecard is a tracking device used to report business results.
- All teams develop their own scorecards that feed into the company scorecard.
- Because we are all linked, all departments are focused on common goals.
- Action items are developed based on the goals set forth on the team's scorecard. In other words, if "X" is our goal, what is one action we can take to move toward obtaining that goal? (It is important to note that it is not one action that accomplishes the goal, but the cumulative effect of numerous completed actions. It is amazing how something that starts out as almost an unattainable goal can be achieved by chipping away at it.)

- Scorecards change over time, along with strategic goals, but are typically set for the year. That's not to say that the same objective might not remain on the scorecards for several years! Whatever is needed to get to lasting improvements.

Process Based Leadership follows a unique communication process to address the need for consistent communication. This is accomplished through the Business-Focused Team (BFT) meetings:

- Everyone is busy on operations, so only two 30-to-60-minute "business-focused" meetings are required each month.
- There is a set agenda centered around the team scorecard.
- Each team has its own action register to document assigned action items.
- Everyone must attend their home BFT meeting.
- Issues discussed during the meeting must be business-driven and related to the scorecard.

The Accountability Process — Action Register

- An action register is an accountability tool used to document action items, which are tasks that must be accomplished to address scorecard objectives.
- The action register identifies the task to be accomplished, ownership, target dates, number of extensions, completion date, and comments regarding the outcome.
- Action items are required to address scorecard items which fall below the target goal.
- Documented action items serve to verify that what we agreed to complete was completed.

Todd points out, "We could have brought the consultants in to entirely implement PBL, but we rejected that idea in favor of doing it ourselves. Shane Yount was very accommodating. He came to Glastender to train our entire management team and returned a couple times to help us when we needed guidance during our implementation.

"Basically, we had our central purpose statement, guiding values, strategies, and targets already in place. We simply hadn't looked at them as part of a scorecard. Our three-to-five-year goals were centered around quality and efficiency and we were really invested in recording metrics."

Kim noted, "Shane was a great consultant. He didn't force his program on us but gave us the guiding principles that we adapted to our company. The most amazing thing about PBL is how easy the system is. It is not complicated, or difficult to understand, implement, or maintain."

After Shane left, Todd and Kim created a written Process Implementation Plan (PIP) to present to all employees. They told them what they were going to implement and informed them that only management would be using this system at first. Lastly, they explained that once the management team had it successfully implemented, they would be asking all of the employees to participate as well. Kim said, "We had firmly decided that there would be no flavor-of-the-month training at Glastender. If we were to implement new initiatives, we would need to be all-in!

"The real difference was that we now had essential things in place, such as our commitment to quality and efficiency. We also had clear goals and objectives. In fact, when we looked at our scorecard design, we had most of the focus areas already identified from our previous SWOT analysis with Beth McMall."

The Process Based Leadership strategy's main effectiveness lies in carrying out strategic goals. Strategic issues and operational issues are intertwined, but in general, strategic thinking is more long-term in focus:

- Strategy tends to focus on the effectiveness of what is being done, rather than the simple need to get work completed. For example, thinking about doing a quote is an operational concern. Thinking about how rapidly quotes get finished or how many quotes turn into orders is a strategic concern.
- Focus, urgency, and accountability are naturally a part of day-to-day operations, but the need exists to have that same focus, urgency, and accountability in everyone's strategic thinking.

- Process Based Leadership, which Glastender calls Business-Focused Teams, is a process that helps the management team get the entire company aligned to focus on and accomplish strategic goals.
- The transition to a more professionalized, engaged workforce culture has produced increased profitability, greater market share, a loyal customer base, and an engaged workforce that enjoys sharing in business profits.

Recognizing the value of a strong culture should not suggest that strategy and systems are not important. Generating wealth can appear to be boring. You establish a system and simply do it repeatedly. The system's focus takes away from the finger pointing and blaming that occurs when the system is weak or non-existent.

Once a good system is in place, excellence becomes the norm. That's what I discovered when I worked with the National Football League and NASCAR teams. The winning teams have systems that make excellence the norm — an expectation — an on-going habit. Great coaches eliminate finger pointing and the blame-game.

Strategic and systems excellence were on display as I toured the offices, display areas, and the high-tech manufacturing facility at Glastender. The office area is as quiet as a library, with people efficiently executing their responsibilities. The mood is one of positive expectancy — lots of orders being filled, and yet there is no sense of anxiety or stress.

The display area glistens with stainless steel bar equipment that sets the standard for the food equipment industry. The manufacturing area hums with the sounds of robotics shaping products for the growing client base. Surprisingly, the manufacturing area is Disney-World-clean. There is a sense of calm purpose to everything that goes on. There is no crisis mode. Management's practice of focusing on what is important and not urgent keeps Glastender from falling into the urgent *and* important trap that many businesses are forced to cope with.

Based on my own consulting experience, I can make the following assessments: First, in the work I have done with automotive industry giants such as Chrysler Corporation, Ford Motor Company, and General Motors, none of them work as smoothly and efficiently as

Glastender does. I am not downplaying the systems and structure at those very complex and successful companies. I am simply saying that Glastender has a culture and systems worth emulating as a best practice manufacturing model.

Second, Glastender's leadership team has created what great teams in any business do: It has established a cadence wherein each newly-designed product is built and quickly replicated. Orders are received and shipped via a system that works like a well-oiled machine. Employees are fully engaged and push the envelope because they share in the profits generated by their individual and collective contributions to the productivity and profitability of the business that employs them.

Glastender's second-generation leadership team has fostered a true family-feel to the business, seeing all employees as a part of the family business. This team has truly changed the game.

Chapter Twelve

GAME CHANGER: OPEN BOOK MANAGEMENT

The second serious game changer that really helped shape a better culture and drive productivity at Glastender was Open Book Management, based on the book *The Great Game of Business* by Jack Stack.

According to Kim, "To explain the genesis of Open Book Management, we had an underlying goal for Glastender to be the *employer of choice,* especially in manufacturing. The image of working for the large automotive companies still was a draw for employment due to higher wages. We were convinced that if we made our work environment really special, we could attract and keep the best manufacturing talent. An important part of that was to have a meaningful bonus system — one where individual performance is tied to the results produced by the company. Todd's belief is that if you have a bonus system and your people don't know how it relates to their performance, the bonuses are seen as 'pennies from heaven.' People need to see how they can impact the company's bottom line."

Open Book Management (OBM) involves sharing financial information with employees. The concept of OBM is much more encompassing than simple profit sharing. Any company can decide, after having a good year, that they want to share some profits with their employees. OBM involves a much higher level of employee engagement.

The three main tenets of OBM are as follows:

1. Employees are taught how a business makes money ("the rules of the game").
2. Employees are expected to use this knowledge to make decisions.
3. Employee have a direct stake in the company's success by earning bonuses based on profitability.

Under the OBM system, the company starts each year with a financial plan — a predetermined system that clearly identifies for all employees what they expect to achieve based on sales forecasts. Weekly operating statements are shared with all employees, which show how the business is performing compared to the plan for the year. The goal is to beat the financial plan and the resulting profits are shared with employees through a bonus program.

OBM creates a "meaningful" bonus program, because employees know in advance what is possible and what they can do to help. A true OBM system leads to greater company financial performance, because everyone knows what makes the company successful and is focused on making those things happen.

Under the OBM system, there is more focus on financial statements with budgeting, monitoring, planning, and forecasting becoming much more critical. It is desirable to have employees involved in all these processes, but this does not necessarily mean that all employees have knowledge of every expense. For example, OBM does not require the sharing of salary information. The system is tailored to each individual company but is designed to allow all employees to see all the way down to the bottom line profit.

Glastender's management team is responsible for developing the regular reports that are communicated to employees. For example, each week an operating statement (a condensed version of the income statement) is shared with all employees so they are always aware of the overall company performance. In addition, each team has daily and weekly critical numbers that allow departments to gauge their contribution to the overall success of the company.

Todd explains, "How we made OBM happen wasn't easy. The first year of OBM, we lost money as a business because it was 2009, which was when the big recession hit the country. However, we credit OBM for helping us significantly minimize our losses and navigate the next few years. Despite feeling the affects of the recession from 2009 though 2011, our company was profitable and paying out bonuses in the second year of OBM." For Glastender, OBM complimented PBL described in the previous chapter. Todd and Kim both recognize these two management practices as critical to the company's success.

Todd first got exposed to the concept of OBM around 2003. It was an article in the *Federation of Independent Businesses* magazine that summarized the book, *The Great Game of Business*. Kim bought the book and Todd had read the first chapter but then laid it down. "I was not receptive at the time and felt we were not ready."

According to Todd, "In 2006 and 2007, the cost of stainless steel, our largest material expense, had doubled. Our people had gotten used to automatic raises every year. We were losing money, so I told the employees that raises would be delayed. I failed, however, to fully explain our fiscal situation."

In 2007, the union issue reared its head again. Fliers showed up. This time it was the United Steelworkers. An employee brought one to Kim's attention. Kim immediately engaged the services of a consultant to conduct an employee survey right away.

Kim explains, "What happened next was truly unique. Our employees took it upon themselves to contact the National Labor Relations Board (NLRB) to say, 'We have collected signatures from employees saying they don't want the Steelworkers organizers around here trying to organize us.' They were asking, 'What can we do?' The NLRB representative told the employee, 'I don't know, we've never been asked that before!'"

Todd went on to say, "The bottom line was there was some frustration about employees not getting their usual raises. This prompted me, in the fall of 2007, to meet with all employees. I apologized profusely for not having explained the reasons behind the delayed pay raises, as I should have. I proceeded to share our income statement with all employees and said, 'Here's the deal. I didn't explain well enough why we were delaying the raise. The reason is, we lost $600,000 and can't afford the raise.'

Sharing the income statement and showing employees our expenses was an eye-opening experience, which allowed them to understand our situation and see how something outside of our control (the steel market) was impacting the company."

By the beginning of 2008, Todd returned to *The Great Game of Business*, read it completely, and announced to the management team that Glastender would move to OBM at the start of 2009. As part of the preparation, Kim and Todd decided to attend the Gathering of the Games conference presented by the Great Game of Business in St. Louis, Missouri. During the conference, they met Steve Wilson, of Willow Creek Consultants in Hayden, Idaho. He was talking about the process of how to do a bucket bonus. He agreed to do some consulting with Todd. At the conference, they also hired a Great Game of Business consultant to come to Glastender to train the management team.

Following the training, Todd conducted financial literacy training classes with all the employees (classes that he continues to teach with all new employees). In addition, sixty employees volunteered to serve on the expense committees engaging in a process of combing through accounts to identify ways Glastender might save money. For example, one group of employees discovered that buying several types of gloves from many different suppliers was not efficient, nor were the right gloves being worn for the right reason. Revisiting the process of eliminating duplication resolved this redundancy and saved the company money. Another problem was that Glastender had approximately $52,000 of small parcel shipping expenses per year incurred as the result of items missing from initial product shipments. The organization focused on implementing actions to reduce this unnecessary expense to nearly nothing!

Todd comments, "The funny thing was, while we lost money the first year we implemented OBM, we discovered a surprising benefit to the OBM process. Specifically, this process prepared us for the tough times by giving us an incredible fiscal discipline as well as a great communication tool to share information with our employees.

"Finally, our investment in engaging our people through OBM and PBL processes has helped us maintain and strengthen our family culture, benefiting everyone. As a prime example, our profits are four to eight times greater than they were before implementing PBL and OBM. This has allowed us to strengthen our company, pay millions of dollars in bonuses to our employees, and give almost one million dollars to charitable organizations in our community over the last five years."

Chapter Thirteen

SHADOW RODS, LLC.

Jon's Other Passion

When I talk with Jon about his street rods or customizing of production cars, he exudes passion. Even more than that, he radiates a deep understanding and knowledge that goes well beyond that of most car buffs. Normally a man of few words and little appreciation for small talk, when it comes to chatting about his most enduring passion, Jon is effusive.

In discussions with Jon, three themes emerge:

- His car collection is not a distraction from his role as CEO of Glastender, Inc. His inventive work on his cars has, on many occasions, produced ideas and technologies applicable to Glastender's design and manufacturing capacities.
- Engagement in The Motor City Hot Rod Club and with other hot rod enthusiasts has given Jon a lifelong friendship base with people who share kinship for all things related to hot rods and collectable cars.
- Jon has entered Shadow Rods into the manufacturing business.

Reflecting on when Jon and I were in high school, I remember how Jon and a few of his friends got deeply interested in modifying their cars to simply make them into cooler rides or to engage in street drag racing. Jon was a true pioneer in the domain of modifying cars for curb appeal, speed, and safety.

In my case, the first car I ever bought was a powder blue 1956 Bel Air Chevy that someone had already modified. I did not have the creative talent to do any of that. This car was pretty to look at, but it couldn't get out of its own smoke when it came to drag racing.

Jon's first foray into modifying cars started with what he refers to as his "little kid fantasies." For example, when he was only ten years old, he would go to grocery stores and collect orange crates, apple crates, and lettuce crates. He collected different sized crates so he could design and build model cars that more closely resembled the real thing.

In building his model cars, the first thing he would do is find or make a flat board ten inches wide and four feet long. He used this board to create a frame for the structure of his car. Jon would then nail boards crossways to the ends of the plank so he could attach the axels and wheels he had removed from a wagon. He would then set the car on its wheels and place the larger lettuce crate at the back and the smaller apple crate up front, so he could slip his legs and feet in that space. He tied ropes to the ends of the axels so he could turn the car left or right by pulling on the rope (picture a jump rope looped around each axel with the ropes passing through holes drilled in the front board with knots tied in a way that the wheels could be turned by pulling either the rope on the left or the rope on the right).

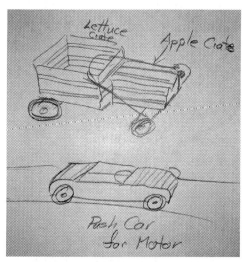

Jon's sketches of his early creations

Jon made several models as shown in these sketches. The first model looks rather like the Model T design while the second depicts a sleeker and faster racing model.

In his preteen years, Reed Draper allowed Jon to hang around the Draper Chevrolet facility, probably because the Draper people knew how much Jon liked cars and because Jon's father had contracted Draper to build refrigerated additions to his trucks. These refrigerated additions enabled drivers to deliver frozen foods.

When Jon showed his sleeker model racecar to Reed Draper, Reed said, "Let's put a motor in that thing." Reed was probably joking, but Jon took him seriously. While this motor offer never materialized, Reed's encouragement further elevated Jon's enthusiasm and strengthened his resolve to continue building or modifying cars that would impress a serious car guy like Reed Draper.

Jon's interest in all things cars, and especially hot rods, truly blossomed during his teen years. To increase his knowledge of hot rods, Jon became an avid researcher. For example, as early as 1953 (at the age of thirteen), he would purchase magazines that were dedicated to articles and pictures of early hot rods. Jon liked the looks of these cars and envisioned designing models of his own.

Jon also avidly studied the history related to the restoration and modification of hot rods and older car engines and bodies for speed.

I asked Jon to elaborate on what he had learned from his research that so inspired his interest in building hot rods and customizing cars. Jon answered from a historical perspective. To paraphrase, this is what Jon told me:

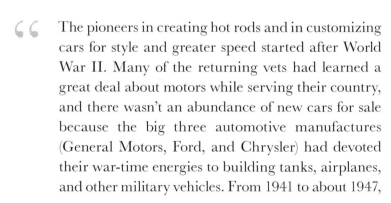

> The pioneers in creating hot rods and in customizing cars for style and greater speed started after World War II. Many of the returning vets had learned a great deal about motors while serving their country, and there wasn't an abundance of new cars for sale because the big three automotive manufactures (General Motors, Ford, and Chrysler) had devoted their war-time energies to building tanks, airplanes, and other military vehicles. From 1941 to about 1947,

car manufacturers stayed with the 1941 models. Furthermore, most of the vets couldn't afford to buy a new car when they completed their military responsibilities, so fixer-uppers became the norm for these young men. Vets favored modifying cars like the '27 Model T, and the Model A '32s and '34s.

The vets who returned to California began to soup-up regular production cars and race just for fun (or for wagers) on dry lake beds that provided flat, smooth surfaces. The flathead V-8 was the motor of choice. To increase the speed and add horsepower to these motors, car buffs added new parts and made other modifications to the engines."

This elaboration provided by Jon yielded me with new insights and a sense of awe. His vivid explanation of the West Coast approaches to modifying cars reminded me of James Stark's customized '53 Mercury in the movie *Rebel Without a Cause*. That movie really put a spotlight on how cool various models of cars could be made to look and perform as street drag racers. Terms like *chopping* and *channeling* became by-words of this new custom car trend that continues today.

Jon explained how the western and eastern parts of the United States took different approaches: "While car guys on the west side of the United States focused on hot rods and drag racing, those on the east side focused mostly on stock car racing on dirt and asphalt ovals on weekends. The stock car guys had to focus on and be ready to compete at weekend events. The street rod guys, on the other hand, could work on their cars anytime they had time to do so. For a guy like me, who works twelve hours a day or more, this was the only option. With a stock car, you can get one up and running quickly and work on it just before a race. This is not possible with street rods."

Jon adds, "Sometimes the guys in the customizing game would lower the back end so low that it was a good idea to equip the car with what are called 'taildraggers.' A taildragger prevented the car from bottoming out when going up a hill. I had a '40 Ford, painted beige and lowered with fender skirts. I installed a taildragger that would keep the car off the pavement when I drove the car down Woodward Avenue as a participant in the Woodward Classic Car Show and Dream Cruise."

Thinking back, I (Don) remembered that the Saginaw area had people fully engaged in both stock cars and street rods. Among the more well-known stock car racers were Cy Fairchild of Saginaw and Johnny Roberts of Breckenridge. Johnny Roberts drove Allison's Shell Service stock car for my uncle, Jack Allison, that won fifty-three features one year. Guys like Jon Hall and Howard Greenwald opted for street rods. Ed Kartz and others chose to focus their efforts on customizing regular production cars.

Jon tied his growing interest in speed to some very practical historical applications that go beyond racing. For example, speed was critical to the bootleggers in the '30s as they tried to outrun the sheriffs. The success of these bootleggers was brought to light with the highly visible successes of infamous bank robbers Bonnie and Clyde. This dangerous duo drove a '32 Ford four-door Deluxe equipped with a flathead V-8 that could go up to 75 miles per hour — much faster than the standard police cars.

Clyde Barrow's preference for Fords with their powerful flathead V-8 motors (always favored, and now re-invented by Jon) led Clyde to write a handwritten letter addressed to Ford Motor Company, dated April 13, 1934. This notorious endorsement read as follows:

" Dear Sir,

While I still have breath in my lungs, I will tell you what a dandy car you make. I have drove Fords exclusively when I could get away [from the police] with one. For sustained speed and freedom from trouble the Ford has got every other car skinned, and even if my business hasen't been strickly legal it don't hurt anything to tell you what a fine car you got in the V8.

Yours truly,
— CLYDE CHAMPION BARROW

Clyde was a criminal, not a spelling bee champion. "Get away" were the operative words in Clyde's letter that is in the possession of the Henry Ford Museum in Dearborn, Michigan.

It is perhaps interesting to note that in 1911, Saginaw's Ray Haroun won the inaugural Indianapolis 500 race at an average speed of 74.602 miles per hour. The cars in that race were clearly able to go much faster at top speed than Clyde Barrow's Ford sedan.

Once Jon was out of the military, when he enrolled in Saginaw High School night classes, he encountered a classmate named Larry Fairchild, brother of stock car race driver Cy Fairchild. In mid-winter, Larry drove a hot rod with no fenders to the school because that was the only car he had to drive. But Larry also owned a '27 Ford Model T roadster body that Jon had seen before he entered the service. Jon offered Larry $50 for the roadster body. Larry took the deal. Jon's passion for working on '27 Model T roadsters was off and running.

After Jon purchased the body of this 1927 Ford Roadster for $50, he did all of the body work in the basement of Jon and Brenda's first house, turning it into a drivable vehicle a year later.

Jon knew he had unusual ability to soup up and customize hot rods and production cars. He was especially interested in modifying '27

Model T roadsters. However, Jon acknowledges that, "had Larry's '27 roadster been a '32 or '34 Model A, my passion probably would have leaned toward those models because at that time, most people wanted the '32 Ford Model A for racing because it was easy to remove the fenders and running boards and to reinstall after a race. The '34 Model A didn't fare quite as well because it had fenders that were more difficult to remove and reinstall."

Jon's progress on building his own hot rod model follows a pathway from prototype to production. He pays attention to every detail. That makes his self-named "Time Tunnel T" truly a work of art.

Jon's 1927 Ford as it is today, the "Time Tunnel T"

Jon further explains that he saw many needed changes to the '27 Model T design. "One problem I saw with the '27 model was its size. It was really small and could only comfortably accommodate people of short stature and I was six feet tall. And there were other challenges. The car had a steering wheel that was set at a 70-degree angle and a seat positioned high above the floorboard. These things were necessary at the time because in those days there was no power steering and drivers needed to apply a lot of strength to simply turn the wheel. The high seats enabled greater leverage. The steering wheel was really big, and the windshield also stood very tall."

To make cars more aerodynamic, hot-rodders would lower the car over the frame (called channeling); lower the seat that hosted the driver; and reduce the height of the front window (called chopping) to reduce wind resistance. In combination, these changes accommodated the growing need for speed.

Around 2000, Jon realized there was much to be done if his '27 roadster was to accommodate his six-foot-tall body and be comfortable and safe enough to drive on streets and highways. Quoting Jon, "I decided to try to make the '27 Model T fit on a '32 frame and to use the '32's grill and gas tank." Once completed, he took the car to the Autorama car show and was awarded third place.

Jon needed a facility and machinery to facilitate all he wanted to do. Prior to affording his own facility and very expensive tools, Jon had rented space at the Bay City Body Shop for $1.00 per hour. The rent included the use of their tools. To be able to buy his own tools, it would have been necessary to pay upwards of $1,000 just to get started.

As Glastender's profits improved, Jon was able to save enough from his earnings to buy his needed tools — always being careful to keep Glastender and his work on cars separate. As his Glastender facility was expanded, Jon chose to build his own facility on that property to work on his cars.

There proved to be a valuable connection between Glastender and Jon's work on building hot rods and customizing cars. Why? Because Jon's work on designing and customizing his cars frequently unleashed technologies that would translate into viable applications to the design and manufacturing of Glastender products.

While continuing to grow the Glastender business, Jon was busy after hours, designing, building, and modifying a variety of hot rods, cars, and trucks for himself. People liked what they saw, and Jon began to believe that he could build cars that others would like to buy from him.

In 2001, Jon created Shadow Rods, LLC. because, "I was at a point where I wanted to build cars for other people. I called it Shadow Rods because everything I build is a shadow of the original. I started with my plan to enhance the lines and make a '27 Ford model of my own design that is bigger, safer, and more comfortable. I wanted to manufacture stamped bodies, built to my specifications, for others to use as a foundation."

It is important to note that Jon has had some very capable help along the way in building Shadow Rods into the creative gem it is today. Paul Behling is Shadow Rods's business manager. He has been working as a key player on the Shadow Rods team for ten years — joining Shadow Rods in 2009 to help get it off the ground. Paul says, "It was an easy decision joining hands with Jon. He and I have been working now together for ten years, and each and every day is a joy. Working with someone who has such a creative mind, a vision for doing things differently and better, and still loving the projects as well as the finished vehicles — that is a joy! I hope both Jon and Rods live on well into the future because this man has done stuff for the hot rod industry like no other — just as he has done for the food equipment manufacturing industry. Both legacies should move on."

Mark Kirby is Shadow Rods's engine development engineer. He is the third member of the Shadow Rods team and is seen by all as a major contributor to Shadow Rods's all new aluminum flathead V-8 engine.

Mark reflects on how he joined Shadow Rods with this poignant story: "In 2008, I was diagnosed with kidney cancer. I was in business for myself and I had no insurance. Jon graciously put me on his payroll and got me insured. The cost of my operation was covered. He literally saved my life!"

The Shadow Rods team of Jon, Paul, and Mark is driven by a passion for cars, engines, and especially hot rods. They love what they do, and they love one another. Quite a team, indeed.

Jon met Keith Crain at a car show over twenty years ago. At the time he had no idea who he was — the CEO of Crain Communications in Detroit, Michigan and publisher of *Automotive News* and *Auto Week*. They simply talked a lot about cars. Just cars. Jon admires Keith's ability to express a completely different point of view in a way that makes him interested in learning more, often times changing his own point of view in the process. Jon also respects Keith's business sense and his down-to-earth personality. Keith makes the following observation about Paul and Mark: "Paul and Mark both appear to have lifetime annuities. Jon is the ultimate perfectionist, always five years from being finished with any given project, and Paul and Mark get that."

As a fellow hot rod enthusiast and a close friend of Jon, Keith said, "Jon is the best manufacturing guy in the world. He should be the lead design person for Ford Motor Company or General Motors. However, if he were in such a role, he would be introducing the 1965 Mustang today — but it would be perfect!"

In response to Keith's assessments, Jon has this to say: "To me, the end product is never what I push for or really enjoy. I hate to see projects completed because I so love the process itself. If I let a hot rod or motor project sit for a year or so, new things come on the market that I want to add to further improve the project."

Keith adds, "Hot rods brought Jon and me together. It is a small group of guys who like cars and our club is called 'The Motor City Hot Rods.' Jon is both ambitious and generous with his time and know-how. He adds a lot to this group and is a key factor as to why this club is still functioning today."

What might be the core competence that drives Jon's success?

My observation is that the answer lies in the fact that, like most inventors, Jon thinks in pictures! Thinking in pictures, to my mind, imbues Jon with a special genius that operates almost like a computer. Jon thinks like an artist when he is designing for Glastender products and for his automotive projects. Jon says, "I would rather make things than go on vacation. Some people love to look at what God made. I like to look at what man made." He has the innate ability to actually visualize what he wants to create.

In her book, *Thinking in Pictures,* Temple Grandin reveals, "Thinking in pictures is a mode of perception, of feeling and thought and being, which we may call 'primitive' if we wish, but not 'pathological'. It is a gift that generally goes unrecognized and unexploited in educational institutions."

Chapter Fourteen

JON'S INNOVATIONS

J on has been called an entrepreneur, but one could argue that this is not the true essence of his being. *Dictionary.com* defines an entrepreneur as "a person who organizes and manages any enterprise, especially a business, usually with considerable initiative and risk."

Jon is definitely an entrepreneur, but while he used his initiative to start a business based on his innovative ideas, the fact that he is more than happy to let others handle the operation of the business gives us an indication that entrepreneurship is not his greatest passion.

Merriam-Webster.com says that to invent is "to produce (something, such as a useful device or process) for the first time through the use of the imagination or of ingenious thinking and experiment." Based on this definition, it seems that Jon is more of an inventor than an entrepreneur, even though, obviously, he is both.

As a young entrepreneur, Jon sought the advice and counsel of a patent attorney named John McCulloch. Jon was only 24 years old when he obtained his first patent. John taught him what to look for in a product he was designing to make it patentable. He explained to Jon that how you solve a problem is often the source of your patent. Jon remembers John saying, "I wish I could find some rich inventors!" — a reference to the fact that many inventors never strike it rich or do anything with their patents.

In speaking with Jon's son Todd, we learn that he might characterize his father even more specifically as a disruptive problem solver, especially when the problems involve the physical world. "Between issues at Glastender, building cars, or just solving everyday situations, my dad's mind is almost always dwelling on some sort of physical problem and how to solve it or do it better," says Todd.

Todd goes on to say, "Truth be told, my dad is very stubborn when it comes to innovation. Once he thinks of a new way to do something, it is very difficult to influence his decision making until he has had a chance to try out his ideas. He also becomes very obsessive. He will not stop thinking about it.

"To this day it is still the same. Just a couple of years ago, we flew out to visit a stainless steel fabricator that we were considering purchasing in order to more quickly break into the kitchen fabrication market. While they were pretty good at what they were doing, the facility was definitely not state-of-the-art, and when we left, all my dad could think about was how to fabricate a sink bowl better than what we were seeing at that fabricator or anywhere else in the marketplace."

Jon's son-in-law Mark chimed in on Todd's story: "Yeah, I remember that day very well. Jon and I sat together on the airplane on the way back and I could tell his mental wheels were turning. He just kept staring ahead, with his mind churning, until finally Jon said, 'I've got it!' and when we got back to Saginaw, that is all he could talk about."

"We worked with some consultants back in the nineties," continued Todd, "and I was complaining about how my father just has to make physical prototypes, even when he knows they are not the ultimate solution. I remember one of the consultants saying that my dad was a 'kinetic thinker' and that it really helped him to see, feel, and touch potential solutions. I am not sure if that is the true definition of a kinetic thinker, but it sure seemed fitting for my dad and I never forgot that phrase."

Jon's passion for invention has been ingrained at Glastender and even though Todd says that Jon can be stubborn about his ideas, he is actually pretty good at letting his employees be creative also, and they even challenge his thinking on potential solutions. It is a wonderful dynamic that speaks to the potential future of Glastender, because you can see that Jon has taught his own family, as well as many of the employees throughout Glastender, to be creative and innovative thinkers.

"My dad's stubbornness has served him well," continued Todd, "because even when his ideas went against the grain of the food service industry, he persisted, assuming that ultimately, his better ideas would prevail."

After years of working closely together, the opinions of Frank Pfisterer nicely sum up Jon's work quality and ethic in the following observations:

> I can see that Glastender takes the route of classic American ingenuity when people wanted to make things with really high quality, innovation, and inventiveness. Glastender is still looking to do that. That's their drive. They really want to innovate, and they really stand for quality in all they're doing and it shows in every spectrum of their business. I appreciate that.
>
> So with respect to Jon, it's nice to see that he builds things that he really appreciates. Things were craftsman built. I even see that in his passion projects, like the Flathead engine with the whole body built on that one floor. I've seen some impressive things that Jon has done. I see that translated into how Jon builds and design things at Glastender. There are very, very few companies in the food service arena that, in my opinion, even come close to operating and building products with quality and intention, the way that Glastender does.
>
> I get kind of spoiled with Glastender. It has a tremendous amount of accountability. If something's broken, they're not just looking to kind of shrug it off or to blame the customer. What we see as a standard in our industry is that nobody wants to have accountability. But if a Glastender product is broken, they're going to want to fix it. And that's why so few of their products actually break. Honestly, it's because they've taken the necessary time over the years to manufacture things and build things in a way that makes sense, so their products have longevity.
>
> The only shame of the whole thing is Glastender has created a standard that only exists for them."

Case in point: In the summer of 1970, Monitor Lanes Bowling Alley in Bay City, Michigan had a Glastender glass washer installed in their bar. Owner Don Dodick recently decided to retire the washer after 50 years of constant service, stating, "I hate to see it go!" Of course, they are updating to a newer model of the Glastender glass washer, of which Don says he looks forward to many years of service from the new one.

Jon has been very innovative within the food service equipment industry and developed many industry firsts, but to simply list all of them does not tell the story as well as getting into more detail on a smaller number of them.

Jon started Glastender by inventing the world's first automatic rotary glass washer back in 1969 and then in 1970 sold the first pass-thru cocktail station, but his innovations definitely did not stop there. Jon kept developing new products in a slow but sure quest to be a full-line bar equipment manufacturer.

The very first "cocktail station," installed at
Johnson's Bar in Lansing, Michigan in 1970

In the mid-1980s, Jon started manufacturing back bar refrigerators after purchasing the assets of the Cooler Corporation of America out of Florida that had gone bankrupt manufacturing single-door keg coolers. Consider the competitive landscape at the time: True Manufacturing and Beverage Air were both already manufacturing back bar coolers, but they were kind of like the "Henry Fords" of the back bar cooler world; you could have any cooler you want as long as it is black. They built coolers for inventory and had them in stock at distributors all over the country. To Jon's way of thinking, their dimensions did not really make sense. For example, their two-door coolers were roughly 59" wide by 29" deep by 37" high.

Keep in mind, neither True nor Beverage Air manufactured stainless steel underbar. They specialize in refrigeration and so it seems they do not worry about whether or not their cooler dimensions mate well with the rest of the equipment in the bar.

The other major competitor at the time was the Perlick Corporation out of Wisconsin, which was founded in 1917, so they had a 52-year head start on Glastender. Since Perlick was already a full-line bar equipment manufacture, Jon viewed them as Glastender's chief competitor, and their two-door cooler was 63-3/4" wide by 23-9/16" deep by 37" high.

Since Jon already manufactured stainless steel underbar and was regularly designing complete bar layouts, he felt that the cooler dimensions were too important to take lightly. He agreed with Perlick that coolers should be 24" deep, because stainless steel underbar lineups most often end up at 24" deep and this would allow any cooler to be front-flush with the lineup, although Jon took it a step further by recessing the back of the cooler compressor compartment so that you could plug the unit in behind the compressor and still push the unit flush against the wall.

For the left-to-right dimensions, Jon disagreed with everyone. He liked Perlick's 24"-wide doors and thought that made sense, but he wanted a 12"-wide compressor compartment, whereas Perlick's compressor compartment was 15-3/4" wide. It turns out that Perlick arrived at their 15-3/4" dimension because they used a pre-manufactured condensing unit and that was as small as the compressor compartment could get and still fit the condensing unit.

One of the first keg coolers circa 1985

In order to get his 12"-wide compressor compartment, Jon decided to build his own condensing unit by purchasing the compressor, condenser coil, condenser fan, and related parts, and assembling his own condensing units right at the Glastender factory. Jon was very pleased, because with his 24"-wide doors and 12"-wide compressor compartments, he had two-, three-, and four-door back bar coolers in very predictable, design-friendly lengths of 5', 7', and 9', even for self-contained units and remote unit lengths (i.e., units without an on-board condensing unit) of 4', 6', and 8' even.

Jon's obsession with getting it just right did not end there. Next, he took aim at the height of back bar coolers. As mentioned, True and Beverage Air were 37" high and in addition, they only offered their back bar coolers with a finished top. Since Jon wanted to be able to offer his coolers without a finished top for an integrated style back bar when the customer is supplying their own bar top above the cooler, he disregarded True and Beverage Air.

Perlick's back bar coolers were available without a finished top (at the time — in more recent years, they have changed and only provide their coolers with a finished top also), which Jon liked, but he still did not understand their dimensions. Perlick's cabinet was 37" high, but back bar tops are usually 42" high, so once you subtract about an inch for the top thickness, that left a 4" gap between the top of the cooler and underside of the back bar top.

Some locations would build a 4" curb to set the coolers on and that would take up the 4" gap, but there were many places that preferred their coolers on legs, which meant Perlick had to supply them with 4" legs. Jon's strong understanding of the National Sanitation Foundation (NSF) standards meant he understood that health departments require a minimum of 6" legs to ensure enough clearance between the bottom of the cooler and the floor for proper cleaning. It seems that Perlick might have gotten around this by always supplying a kick rail with their legs, but regardless of that, Jon was determined to have a 35"-high cabinet so that he could supply 6" legs to achieve the necessary overall height of 41".

Jon was in a bit of a quandary though. In the food service industry, when one manufacturer gets specified on a project (i.e., designed into a job), in order for another manufacturer to bid on the job, they must be able to match the other manufacturer's critical specifications and Jon was worried that Perlick's 37" cooler cabinet height might be one of those critical specifications. He reasoned that Glastender coolers did not have to match the length, because extra space that way is not normally an issue, and in fact might be a benefit, but not matching the height would be a problem if the job site had a 4" curb, because then the Glastender cooler would be 2" too short.

Jon solved this problem by designing his coolers with a main cabinet and a separate channel-base that attached to the cabinet. He offered the base in 1"-high or 3"-high models. The 1" base worked where Glastender was specified and the 3" base worked where Perlick was specified.

If you think there are a lot of details to this back bar cooler story, then you are getting a glimpse into the mind of Jon Hall and how much he thinks about all of the details. And the story is not over yet, because after we fast-forward a few years, we get to see the real impact that Jon and his start-up Glastender had on the industry.

Glastender had been growing nicely in the early nineties and by 1995, Jon no longer felt the need to offer the 3" base on Glastender coolers. In his new design, the base was integrated with the cooler and the overall height of the cabinet was always 35".

In a sign that Jon's thoughts on cooler cabinet dimensions made sense and that Glastender was having an impact on the industry (i.e., growing and getting specified more), by 1997, Perlick released a new line of back bar coolers that had a 12"-wide compressor compartment and the overall height of the cabinet was now set at 34-1/2" instead of 37". In Perlick's defense, the 12" compressor compartment was probably made necessary by the fact that Glastender often designs their layouts to be tight (i.e., no extra space), so if Perlick wanted to quote against Glastender, they needed to be able to match Glastender cooler dimensions. In all fairness, Glastender has had to match some of their product innovations also, although Glastender has been copied a lot.

In another sign of Jon's influence on the industry, even True and Beverage Air, who are not really known for being flexible, ended up releasing back bar cooler models that more closely matched Glastender dimensions.

For another example of the quality of Jon's thinking and his impact on the industry, we can look at a concept he originated called Modular Bar Die. When you walk up to a bar to order a drink, you lean against the bar top and most likely your knees are touching the wall that holds up the bar top. This wall is called the bar die.

The fabled story behind Jon's invention of Modular Bar Die is that Jon and Jay Kegerreis were at a club, sitting at the bar and having a drink. Jon left to use the rest room and when he returned he told Jay that he felt like they should take their drinks and hang out in the bathroom, because the beautifully tiled bathroom smelled better than the bar.

Apparently, Jon felt that the source of the bad smell was the bar die wall. Bar die walls were normally made of wood and often the spills and excess moisture behind the bar would seep into the wall, leading to an "off" smell over time.

And with that, Jon came up with the idea for Modular Bar Die, where Glastender would build the bar die wall out of 16"-gauge galvanized steel studs and then cantilever the stainless steel underbar (sinks, ice bins, drainboards, etc.) off the wall so that the bartender-side was stainless steel from the floor to the underside of the bar top and there were no legs on the underbar, making it very easy to keep clean.

Jon's Modular Bar Die

Glastender installed its very first Modular Bar Die job in Ohio in 1990, and as fate would have it, Perlick would unveil their very own version of Modular Bar Die that same year. Since Perlick was quicker on the draw with marketing material, it appeared to some people that they had released it before Glastender.

If you review Perlick's original brochure, you can tell that their thinking was different than Jon's. They eliminated many of the underbar legs (for some reason, normal underbar was mounted to the wall, but cabinet-style underbar was still on legs), but at the same time, they provided a platform held up by legs that held the entire bar die wall off the floor. Consequently, they did not eliminate the legs and they also did not have the stainless steel bar die sealed to the floor to prevent moisture from getting to the millwork panels finishing the customer-side of the bar.

Interestingly enough, the owners of Glastender and the owners of Perlick are on friendly speaking terms. Yes, they are fierce competitors, but they also have a lot of respect for each other as well as a shared understanding of what it is like to manage a family business. Consequently, the managers of the two companies tend to get reacquainted every time there is a new North American Association of Food Equipment Manufacturers (NAFEM) trade show.

At the 1997 NAFEM show in Dallas, Texas, Perlick introduced their all-new Modular Bar Die design, and in a nod to Jon, Larry Molinari, president of Perlick at the time, told Jon and Todd that their new modular bar die design was a copy of Glastender's design with a couple new features that Glastender would likely want to add. One of those features was leveling feet, which Jon had contemplated and decided would not work well, and he must have been correct, because Perlick eliminated that feature a short time later. The second was a beer line chase created by severing all of the bar die uprights to create a pocket to accept the beer lines and then covering it with removable plate. Perlick still has that feature to this day, but Jon questioned whether or not it affected the integrity of the wall and Glastender never did copy the feature.

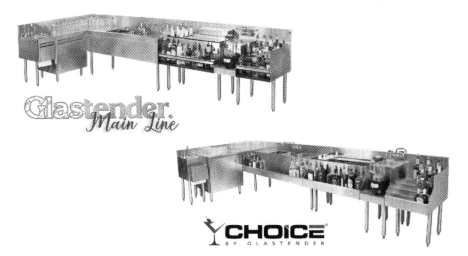

The current underbar lineup

In a testament to the soundness of Jon's original design, the only thing that has really changed on his original bar die wall is the chaseway hole pattern in the vertical studs. Otherwise, the version sold today is the same as what was originally invented in 1990, and Jon's basic design has become the industry standard, with other manufacturers also releasing versions that are essentially copies of Jon's design.

Refrigeration equipment lineup

The examples above help to illustrate the incredible amount of consideration that Jon puts into his product development projects. This only scratches the surface of the extent of Jon's innovations over the years, because for him, it often seems there is no detail that is too small to consider.

Chapter Fifteen

REWARD OUTWEIGHS RISKS

Contributed by: Rejeana Heinrich, Director of the Stevens Center for
Family Business, Saginaw Valley State University

I *have gained a great deal of insight into family-owned and -operated business*
by consulting with the founders, administrators, and staff of such enterprises
across a range of issues, such as succession planning, strategic planning,
communication, leadership development, and team building. Teaching Family
Business and Entrepreneurship at Saginaw Valley State University has brought
even greater insight and appreciation for this major segment of the U.S. economy.
However, in thinking about this chapter, I turned to Rejeana Heinrich, the director
of the Stevens Center for Family Business at Saginaw Valley State University. This
bright and dedicated lady lives and breathes family business.

This is what Rejeana has to say.

* * *

Family businesses are complicated. Not only must they meet all the
challenges and demands of any business, but they must also manage
the intricate — sometimes treacherous — terrain of family relationships
and dynamics.

Family-owned enterprises are ubiquitous. In fact, there are 5.5
million family businesses in the United States; family firms comprise

80% to 90% of all business enterprises in the U.S. With their significant impact on the GNP, employment, and new job creation, it's apparent that family-based business is the bedrock of the country's economy. The greatest part of America's wealth lies with family-owned businesses.

It's not unusual for people to think that family business means small business. Not true! In fact, 60% of the publicly-held U.S. companies are family-controlled. Wal-Mart, Ford Motor Company, Koch Industries, Cargill — these are some of the largest family businesses in the U.S.

What these iconic companies have in common with the mom-and-pop shop on the corner, with the small manufacturing firm in the community's industrial park, and with enterprises as diverse as *Rolling Stone* magazine and the Grand Hotel on Michigan's Mackinac Island, is the family element — the owners and decision-makers have the unique relationship of being bonded by blood and by marriage.

The perspective of family businesses (FBs) is generational. Their goal is the perpetuation of the enterprise for decades and centuries to come, with the founding family retaining its principal place in ownership, governance, and control.

While generating wealth for the family is fundamental, FBs typically have additional aspirations and goals by which they define their success or failure. These non-financial outcomes can range from family cohesion and happiness to psychological meaning and identity to family image, prestige, and legacy — aspects of value that can't be measured with dollar signs and decimal points.

In fact, social-emotional wealth is increasingly being identified as a hallmark characteristic that differentiates family businesses from non-family businesses. While executives and employees of non-family enterprises can and certainly do feel a great deal of pride in the companies they work for, and experience a sense of reward that surpasses the paycheck and other perks they receive, research has indicated that they do not feel the deep connection and real sense of "ownership" — literally — that the founders and succeeding generations of family businesses hold for their enterprises. We're all familiar with the truism that when your name is on the storefront, there's an extra sense of connectedness, responsibility, dominion, even identity with the physical/fiscal entity that comprises the company.

It's all of these intangibles that comprise socio-emotional wealth, and in many ways constitute the "secret sauce" that has made family business such a powerful entity within societies and economies around the world.

Regardless of the intangible rewards, it's also notable that family businesses out-perform their non-family counterparts on the traditional measures of success — factors such as revenue growth, ROA (Return on Assets), cash flow returns, EBITDA (Earnings Before Interest, Taxes, Depreciation, and Amortization), EVA (Economic Value Added), and share-price returns. Tracking comparable results by many previous studies by a wide range of investigators, a research report published by Credit Suisse in September of 2017 states, "The financial performance of family-owned companies is superior to that of non-family-owned businesses across the globe."

What accounts for this remarkable difference? Stated simply, it's because family businesses traditionally take the long view toward the management and operations of their enterprises. Their attention is not narrowly focused on the next quarter's financials, but on a much longer horizon. Their goals and objectives are in terms of not just years and or even decades, but of familial generations, with "success" being the successful transfer of ownership to the children and the children's business.

Given the two sometimes-diametrically opposed systems at work within a family business — the family system and the business system — it's almost astonishing that the forces are reconciled, and the outcomes are productive. Consider:

- The family unit is an emotional system — it flourishes in an environment of love and nurturing. An individual is cared for simply because they exist and are part of the family. However, the business system is task-based — the individual's value derives from their function.
- Within the family, the mission is to raise the offspring to be independent, competent adults. Within the business, the mission is to produce profitable goods and services. Equality is the rule within families: Mom and Dad (theoretically) love each child

the same, regardless of their gifts and talents. In a business, competency is valued and rewarded.

• Similarly, acceptance of the individuals within a family is unconditional. In the business, acceptance is based on objective performance.

• Family relationships are permanent. Spouses may get divorced, but not so parents, grandparents, and children— their bonds endure forever. Business relationships are contractual, with employer or employee able to end the relationship at any time.

• Power within families frequently derives from what generation the individual is in, or where they fall within the sibling birth order. In the business world, power is primarily based on authority and influence.

Nevertheless, family businesses can and certainly do wind their way through these conflicting paradigms and create money-making enterprises that satisfy financial goals and objectives while also being personally rewarding and a source of pride to the family members involved.

A fascinating difference between family and non-family businesses is their approach to nepotism: the hiring of family and having direct reporting relationships between family members. In the corporate world, policies against nepotism are standard. A family member may work for the same company, but not within the same department or division. If two members of a work group decide to marry, one of them must leave. Quite reasonably, this is to guard against potential problems such as favoritism, fraud, personal issues being brought into the workplace, or unfair disciplinary practices.

In a family business, the approach is quite the opposite; not only *can* family members work together, but they are cultivated, nurtured, and encouraged to do so.

How can a concept that is so ingrained in one environment — prohibitions against nepotism — be effectively turned on its head and be beneficial for the family business workplace?

A key factor to explain this is the familial relationship itself: Because family members who work together typically have a shared history, the same value system, and many years of intimately communicating with one another, they have a profound basis of mutual understanding which translates into teamwork and common goals and objectives in the workplace.

When family members work together, striving for the success of the family enterprise, there is a higher level of commitment and a real sense of ownership than that which prevails in non-family businesses. These factors lend to higher levels of loyalty and morale, along with greater trust.

On the practical side, looking to the family circle for new employees can also mean lower recruiting costs, lower training costs, and lower employee turnover, because of the shared history; the fact that family members intimately know each other's strengths, weaknesses, aspirations, and motivations; and the commitment and loyalty that family members demonstrate toward the company.

When family business first began to be studied as a distinct entity within the business world, a fascinating statistic emerged: About 30% of all family-owned businesses survive into the second generation, 12% will still be viable into the third generation, with 3% of all family businesses operating at the fourth-generational level and beyond. The initial reaction can be: OMG! So many family businesses going down the tubes!

However, in relative terms, the success rate of family businesses is quite impressive. The average life expectancy of all firms is 12 years, but for family-owned businesses, it's 24 years. Twice as many FBs than non-FBs survive to 30 and 60 years. Firms that are older than 300 years, most are still family businesses.

Family businesses setting longer-term performance horizons translates into many strategic, management, and operating decisions. They are more likely to reinvest in the business, including in their human and capital assets. Research shows more investment in plant machinery and electronic data interface in FBs than non-FBs. Family businesses spend four percent of staff costs on training, versus three percent for non-FBs.

Their longevity is testament to family businesses' resilience. They also demonstrate greater flexibility. A close family network helps with quick decision-making — a strong competitive edge, especially in tough economic times and in the current turbulent environment of fast change.

Family businesses demonstrate many advantages compared to their non-FB counterparts: culture, resilience, knowledge, flexibility. Another significant factor is stability: The tenure of CEOs within family businesses is six times that of non-family-owned businesses.

The same factors, of course, that work to a family business's advantage can become liabilities if not managed wisely. The dangers of nepotism are always looming, unless the FB's values, policies, and procedures are clear and adhered to. The consistency of a long-time CEO can become a detriment if paternalistic practices are carried to the extreme or innovative ideas are thwarted. The close family bonds that allow for trust and effective communication can become tainted by negative interpersonal issues that spill over into the business, creating a corrosion that contaminates the entire culture and workforce.

Therein lies the dilemma of family business leadership and management: how to navigate the complex terrain of family relationships while keeping the business on the path to financial success and long-term viability.

Many family businesses do this by making a fundamental decision based on the answer to this question: Will the enterprise be family first, or business first?

Sounds like a simple, binary choice, right? In fact, most family businesses operate somewhere on the continuum of these two poles, trying to effectively balance the needs of the business and of the family members involved with the business. It is not unusual for the family first/business first perspective to change from time to time, in response to whatever situation the business and/or a family member may be facing.

In a "business first" scenario, the culture and decisions are based on the business priorities and standard operating practices of solid business philosophy. In the dichotomy of the two systems — family and business — presented above, the "business" considerations would prevail.

If a family business opts to be "family first," quite a different approach is taken. The needs, desires, wants, expectations, and motivations of family members are deliberately accommodated within the enterprise.

Key areas where the family first/business first lines may become blurred are:

- Employment of family members in the company — Is being part of the family business a birthright, or does the family member need to meet the same qualifications and criteria for the job as would any other candidate?
- Income and compensation — Are they based on some concept of "equality" among family members, and/or with a premium being paid to family members? Or, is pay for family members based on real market value, and based on the individual's responsibilities and contributions to the business?
- Leadership or promotion — Does the familial birth order dictate who's the "senior" executive? Or, are leadership positions and promotions earned and based on merit?
- Training — Are investments in the individual's professional growth based on that person's position within the family, or on the anticipated return (potential gain or earnings) that the training will result in for the company?
- Perspective and basis of operation — Emotion? Or, task-oriented with the company's best interest being the priority?

In real life, of course, there are rarely clear either/or answers to these questions. The course the family business takes can be any mix of family first/business first and can change given circumstances. It's commonplace to anticipate that second, third, and ongoing by-blood or by-marriage generations will have preference for grooming for top positions — a hallmark of family business is that not only ownership, but leadership roles, will transfer from generation to generation.

Chapter Sixteen

TIME MOVES ON

I have known Jon Hall since fourth grade. That is what I thought — until I wrote this book. I realize now that I had no idea of who the real Jon Hall was. His story reveals a person who is a living, breathing example of what the term *continuous improvement* really means. Each day, as Jon's feet hit the floor, he begins to think about what he can design and build to improve the products and services of Glastender, the world-class food equipment manufacturing business he founded fifty years ago.

Whether looking at Jon through the lens of Glastender or through his hot rod avocation, perfection is a common thread. He loves the process of creating and building. His close friend Keith Crane, when asked to describe Jon, had this to say: "Jon is the best manufacturing guy in the world. He should be the lead design person for Ford Motor Company or General Motors. However, if he were in such a role, he would be introducing the 1965 Mustang today — but it would be perfect!" Why is this true? Because, as Jon says, "I so love the process itself."

Jon in 2005
Portraits by Gregg

Jon is truly authentic — always representing his true nature or beliefs. Whether it is wearing his Levi blue jeans and a tee shirt, or espousing manufacturing as the true backbone of the American economy, what you see is what you get. No pretense or waffling.

Jon teared up as I asked him about his former business partner and best friend, Jay Kegerreis. He smiles brightly when he talks about his adult children (Kimberly, Todd, Richard, and Kristina) and how they have contributed to the growth and profitability of Glastender, Inc. or how his son, Jon Jr., founded his own business, Phat Cat Guitars. Finally, Jon is quick to give kudos to his wife of 55 years, Brenda. He sees her as the heart and soul of the family.

The Hall family in 2017
Hicks Studio

Rebel Without Applause is the title given this book because, despite Jon's personal success and that of his family, he is a relatively unknown quantity in his home town of Saginaw, Michigan, and despite the major role the Hall family and their business continues to play in contributing significant dollars to a multitude of community causes. Perhaps, in some small way, this book will unveil the essence of Jon Hall to future generations of Hall children and to the world at large.

My belief is that in writing a book like this, you never really finish. You simply surrender — with full knowledge that you haven't captured everything there is to say about Jon Hall and Glastender. The combination of a great foundation focused on quality and continuous improvement, a young team of family members at the helm of the business putting productivity systems into place, along with great employees and a loyal customer base will be the cause of continued growth for this energetic company and a very bright future for Jon and Glastender, Inc.

Glastender today
Bublitz Photography

Printed in the United States
By Bookmasters